COPING WITH VENEREAL DISEASE

COPING WITH
VENEREAL DISEASE

GABRIELLE I. EDWARDS

Illustrated by Nancy Lou Gahan

THE ROSEN PUBLISHING GROUP

NEW YORK

Published in 1980, 1983, 1985, 1988 by The Rosen Publishing Group, Inc.
29 East 21st Street, New York, N.Y. 10010

Copyright 1980, 1983, 1985, 1988 by Gabrielle I. Edwards

91- 17806

Revised Edition 1988

Library of Congress Cataloging in Publication Data

Edwards, Gabrielle I
  Coping with venereal disease.

  Bibliography: p.
  SUMMARY: Discusses the history of VD and how it is
contracted and cured.
  1. Venereal diseases. [1. Venereal diseases]
I. Title.
RC200.1.E38   616.95'1   80-11353
ISBN 0-8239-0926-3

57140

Manufactured in the United States of America

This book is dedicated to my
husband, Francis D. Edwards,
who has always encouraged
my writing endeavors.

Photo Credits

Frank Edwards: photocopy of open materials provided by the U.S. Department of Health, Education, and Welfare. Figures 3.2, 3.3, 3.4, 3.5, 3.6, 3.7, 3.8, 3.9, 1.10, 6.1

Alton M. Burton: original photographs. Figures 4.1, 7.2.
C. McLaren and F. Siegel, Burroughs Wellcome Co.: Figure 5.3.
G. Plachta, Burroughs Wellcome Co.: Figures 5.4, 6.2.

Acknowledgments

I express grateful appreciation to the following persons and agencies for contributing to my file of reference research material: Vashti R. Curlin, M.D.; Vernal Cave, M.D.; Center for Disease Control, Atlanta, Georgia; National Cancer Institute, Bethesda, Maryland; the former U.S. Department of Health, Education, and Welfare; Bureau of Venereal Disease Control, New York; Burroughs Wellcome Company, Research Triangle Park, North Carolina; and the U.S. Public Health Service.

About the Author

Mrs. Gabrielle I. Edwards is Assistant Principal Supervision of the Science Department at Franklin D. Roosevelt High School in Brooklyn. She supervises science instruction for 3,200 young people, many of whom have come to live in Brooklyn from countries the world over. This educator/author devotes much of her time and energy to the improvement of educational experiences and opportunities for young people. Her approach to education is based on the philosophy  that at each grade level there must be mastery of the content of prescribed courses of study. In addition, there should always be improvement in the fundamental learning skills of reading, writing, and mathematics. Since reading for both information and pleasure is an important part of a person's life, Mrs. Edwards encourages young people to incorporate reading into their daily life plan. Students are invited to participate in science research activities requiring laboratory skill techniques, reading in depth, and extensive writing.

Mrs. Edwards is the author of several books for students in junior and senior high school, including *Coping with Drug Abuse*, *Biology the Easy Way*, and *Living Things* (co-authored).

Her professional affiliations include active membership in the Biology Chairmen's Association, the New York Biology Teachers Association, the Science Council of New York, the National Association of Biology Teachers, the National Science Teachers Association, and the New York State Science

Supervisors' Association. Each year she coordinates *Science Update*, a workshop/conference for science teachers and supervisors.

Outside of her professional life, Mrs. Edwards is a wife and mother. She has one son. In addition to science writing, she photographs subjects of biological interest.

Contents

Preface

Sometimes it is difficult to talk about things that are private and a bit delicate. There are some secrets that are not easily shared with others, especially those experiences that deal with our intimate lives.

But there are times when we must make exceptions to the unwritten rules of topic taboos, because matters of health and safety require frank and straightforward discussion. Knowing about one's body and learning to prevent disease are of utmost importance to people of all ages. In areas of health knowledge, special attention must be given to the education of the young person. A teenager has the greater part of life before her or him. If during the growing years the body is damaged by disease, the quality of one's adult life is diminished. And, as you will learn from this book, the lives of others can be affected by the mistakes of one person.

There is evidence that anti-intellectual attitudes prevent one from learning scientific truths. Negative attitudes toward learning are expressed by comments such as "The book is too preachy" or "We have the right to do what we want with our body." Let us consider each of these comments. If a book presents platitudes and moralizing without biological data, then it may be considered "preachy." However, if facts are given that clarify the biological processes that take place, there is something to be learned from the author's presentation.

It so happened that during a class period Teacher A distributed books on a particular health problem to a 10th-year class. The actual time of the 40-minute class period was diminished by the time necessary to take attendance and carry out other routine procedures. A teaching time of 30 minutes remained. The books were distributed. Students thumbed through the pages. The books were collected. There was no class reading or focusing in on any one of the book's chapters. When asked how the pupils liked the book, the teacher's comment was that it was "too preachy." The books were not used again.

Teacher B spoke to an 11th-year class about a health problem that concerns teenagers. One boy replied, "It's my body; I can do what I want with it." When questioned, this boy knew nothing about the causative organism of the disease. He knew nothing about the effects of the disease on the body. He had gleaned from hearsay a collection of half-truths and falsehoods, by which he governed his actions.

It will take a great deal of patience on the part of educators to develop willing attitudes in young people that will enable them to learn and accept the biological truths of health situations. A recent poll conducted by a television newscaster pointed out how little sexually active teenagers know about body systems or the causes of venereal diseases. It is indeed unfortunate that curricula in many high schools have been so watered down that young people are not being taught about health and disease.

Many of today's teenagers are sexually active. In far too many instances, the sexual activity begins as early as thirteen or fourteen years of age. By the age of eighteen many sexually involved young people have had numerous sexual encounters with many different partners. The news story shown below illustrates the disastrous health episodes that are caused directly by casual sexual conduct.

REPORT 35,000 PUPILS
GOT VD HERE THIS YEAR

Close to 35,000 "sexually active" teenagers in the city school system have contracted syphilis or gonorrhea this year, State Health Commissioner Robert Whalen disclosed yesterday.

Moreover, 25% of "sexually active" girls in school systems throughout the state end up pregnant, Whalen said. . . .

Addressing a conference on health services to school children, Whalen said teenage sexuality was a high priority in his office. . . .

The purpose of this book is to bring to the young reader the opportunity to explore the biology of diseases that are passed from one person to the next by sexual contact. Knowledge gives us the ability to cope with the realities of life. It is not the author's purpose to pass judgment on behavior or to become philosophical about the subject matter. It is the author's purpose to present knowledge in the clearest fashion possible.

The chapters are arranged so that you can gain increased understanding of the microorganisms that cause venereal diseases: spirochetes, bacteria, viruses. Each of these microorganisms has its own structure and requirements for life, and each affects the body in different ways.

Because AIDS kills so many young people, it has been talked about and written about more than any other disease in modern history. However, the intensive publicity given to AIDS has led many people to believe that other sexually transmitted diseases are no longer present or important. This is not so. Syphilis, gonorrhea, genital herpes, chlamydia, and the others are still harming people. Coping with Venereal Disease is a roll call of known sexually transmitted diseases in the United States.

COPING WITH VENEREAL DISEASE

CHAPTER I

What Is Venereal Disease?

UN REPORTS RAMPANT VD

Venereal disease is rampant among the world's teenagers, and gonorrhea, the most common type, is raging out of control in many countries, the World Health Organization said today. . . . In the United States, there are an estimated 2.5 million cases of gonorrhea. . . . For the world as a whole, the rate of venereal disease among teenagers was twice the rate for the entire population.

Venereal disease is the general name given to a group of diseases. These diseases have one thing in common: they are caused by organisms that are spread from person to person during sexual intercourse or close body contact. Venereal (an adjective that modifies the noun, disease) was derived from the Latin name Venus. As you may know, Venus was the goddess of love in Roman mythology. Since venereal diseases are spread by contact between lovers, they were named for the goddess. The abbreviation VD is given to any or all of these diseases.

There are many venereal diseases. Syphilis, gonorrhea, and genital herpes are the three major ones, because these diseases are the most prevalent and do the most damage. Some other venereal diseases are nonspecific urethritis, trichomoniasis, chancroid, lymphogranuloma venereum, and granuloma inguinale. These are difficult names, but we shall discuss each in turn so that you can understand them.

It is important that we understand the meaning of common terms before we try the difficult ones. To the biologist, disease is an illness that prevents the body from working as it should. Diseases caused by organisms that invade the body are known as infectious diseases. Infectious diseases that are passed from one person to another are called contagious (catching) diseases. The venereal diseases are both infectious and contagious. Each venereal disease is caused by a particular organism. Each causative organism can be passed from one person to another during sexual intercourse or during close body contact involving the sex organs, the rectum, or the mouth.

Fig. 1. shows how one venereal disease, syphilis, was spread from one person to many. Study this chart carefully and note the number of people who became infected with the disease.

Why is there so much concern about venereal disease? There must be concern about a disease that affects so many people. It is estimated that 1.5 million people become infected with one or more of the venereal diseases each year. Although VD is curable, it continues to exist. The rise of VD among teenagers is phenomenal.

Venereal disease is a major health problem among American teenagers. It is estimated that 2,000 teenagers per day are infected with either syphilis or gonorrhea. Over a given year 50 percent of all reported cases of VD occur in persons younger than 25 years of age, and the rate continues to rise among young people. Is there any reason for this condition?

We have said that the venereal diseases are spread through sexual intercourse. It is a fact that today's teenager engages in a kind of promiscuous behavior that makes possible the rapid rise in the incidence of these diseases. The word promiscuous describes behavior that lacks discretion. A promiscuous person is one who has sexual relationships with many people on a casual basis. Since the development of the birth control pill, many teenagers become involved with sex because there is no longer the fear of pregnancy. It is not uncommon for the person of high school age to talk about "doing his or her thing." In most cases, this "thing" turns out to be sexual intercourse. Surprisingly, however, with all their seeming sophistication in matters of sex, young people are very poorly informed about the effects of venereal disease. Before a person can seek medical aid, he or she has to feel the need for such help. If a boy or girl is not aware of the symptoms of the various venereal diseases, a condition may be allowed to go

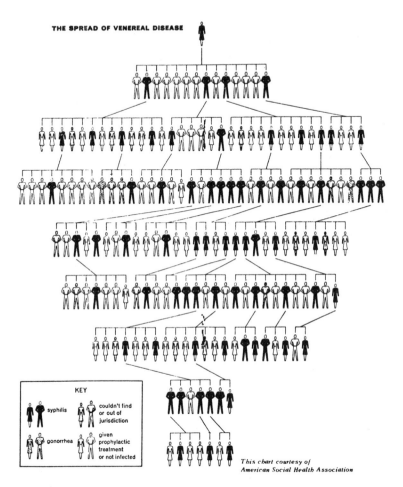

THE SPREAD OF VENEREAL DISEASE

KEY

syphilis

gonorrhea

couldn't find or out of jurisdiction

given prophylactic treatment or not infected

This chart courtesy of
American Social Health Association

Fig. 1. *One infected person can cause a VD epidemic.*

on until complications set in. Promiscuity is not the sole reason for the rise in venereal disease. Improved transportation enables carriers to spread diseases from one geographic area to another in a relatively short time. For example: Mr. Smith has sexual intercourse with a female infected with gonorrhea while he is visiting Country A. Twenty-four hours later he returns to the United States, has intercourse with his non-promiscuous wife, and passes the infection to her. We see that it is not because of her own sexual habits that Mrs. Smith now has VD. Although venereal infections are passed easily from one person to another, it is important to remember that most of these infections can be treated and cured; however, genital herpes and AIDS cannot be cured.

Here are some facts about venereal diseases. They:

> are contagious diseases spread by people who have them;
>
> are transmitted by sexual contact;
>
> are dangerous;
>
> are avoidable by careful living, which includes not having sexual activity with more than one person;
>
> are not preventable by vaccines (none have been developed that provide immunity);
>
> respond to treatment with the exception of genital herpes and AIDS;
>
> can be passed from infected mother to unborn or newborn child;
>
> cause severe damage to the body.

Some Questions to Think About

1. Why should young people learn about venereal disease?
2. From whom should adolescents learn about venereal diseases?
3. Is teaching the truth about disease and infection moralizing?
4. Venereal diseases are now called sexually transmitted diseases. Why is the latter a better name?
5. Why is a promiscuous person a likely source of VD infection?

CHAPTER II

Human Reproductive Systems

Venereal diseases are transmitted from one person to another through sexual contact. The structure of male and female sex organs makes possible physical sexual contact between two persons involving the genitalia of one or both parties. Sex organs are parts of reproductive systems.

A biologist thinks of the human body in terms of systems. A system is a group of organs that work together to perform a certain specialized function. Organs are made up of tissues, and tissues are composed of cells. In order to understand how a system works, one must become familiar with the way in which it is built. This being so, we look at the shape of an organ, note its position in relationship to other organs, and find out about the kind of cells that make up its tissues. Just as types of cells and tissues have names, so do organs. Therefore, understanding requires that we learn the proper names for biological structures. With this in mind, let us turn our attention to a study of the human reproductive systems.

The Male Reproductive System

The function of the male reproductive system is twofold. It produces male sex cells known as sperm, and it provides the means for depositing the sperm where they may fertilize eggs. Before reading further, look at Figure 2.1, a side view of the male reproductive system.

Some organs of the male reproductive system are positioned outside of the body; others are internal. The external organs are known by the general term genitals. The male genitals consist of a penis and two testicles or testes. The testicles are enclosed in a sac called the scrotum. Infected males pass along venereal disease by way of the penis.

The primary function of the testes is to manufacture sperm.

Each testis is composed of thousands of very small tubes called tubules. These small tubes are known as the seminiferous tubules. It is within these tubules that sperm are manufactured. The fact that sperm cells are produced in organs that lie outside of the abdominal cavity is important. For sperm to remain healthy, they must be produced in a temperature slightly lower than body temperature. Once sperm are produced, however, they circulate for a short time in tubes that are inside the body before they are discharged through the penis.

Look closely at Figure 2.2. Note that sperm cells are shown inside of the seminiferous tubules. Between these tubules are

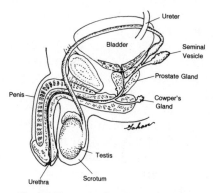

Fig. 2.2 *The male reproductive system.*

groups of interstitial cells. The interstitial cells are very important to the development of mature sperm because these cells secrete testosterone. Testosterone is the male hormone, essential not only for the maturation of sperm cells but also for the development of secondary sex characteristics that takes place with the onset of adolescence. Testosterone stimulates skeletal and muscular growth and causes the growth of pubic hair and the deepening of the voice.

Sperm leave the testis by way of the vas deferens. As the sperm travel through the vas deferens, they pass three glands: the seminal vesicle, the prostate gland, and Cowper's gland. Each of these glands secretes fluids that mix with the sperm. It is believed that these fluids provide nourishment for the sperm, offer protection of a biochemical nature, and facilitate

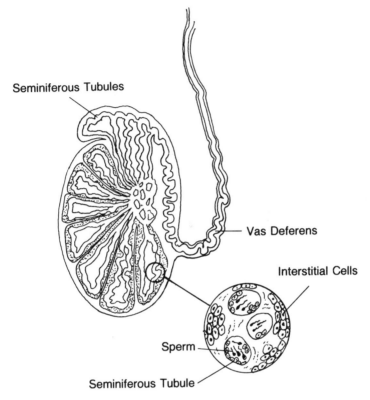

Fig. 2.2 *Longitudinal section of the testis, showing the seminiferous tubules and the interstitial cells.*

swimming movements. The mixture of sperm and these glandular secretions is called semen.

Sperm cells remain in the testes until they are released from the body. A very effective mechanism helps in this release. An increased blood supply that is forced into the capillaries of the penis causes a change in shape of this organ. The penis becomes hard and erect and increases in size. This condition of the penis is known as an erection. Forcible discharge of semen through the urethra and out of the penal meatus is known as ejaculation. Erection of the penis and ejaculation of semen (sperm cells and seminal fluid) are processes essential for the depositing of sperm in the female reproductive tract.

The Female Reproductive System

The female reproductive system has a threefold function. First, female sex cells (ova) are produced. Second, the system processes the ova in terms of either fertilization or disintegration. Third, the developing embryo is protected and given room to grow. All of these functions are carried out by specialized organs that make up the reproductive system.

Of primary importance are the ovaries, two oval-shaped organs that lie on either side of the midline of the body in the lower abdominal region. In humans a mature egg cell is produced each month by a single ovary. The ovaries function on an alternating basis. As an ovum (egg cell) ripens, it bursts out of the follicle in the ovary and is discharged into the appropriate branch of the fallopian tube.

The fate of the ovum that has been released from the ovary is determined by events of the moment. If the egg is fertilized,

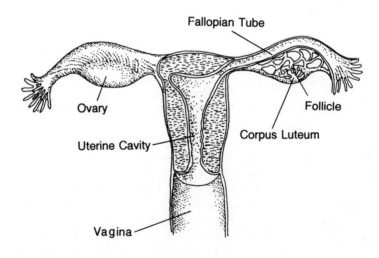

Fig. 2.3. *The female reproductive system.*

it becomes implanted in the uterus, an organ specialized for housing the developing embryo. An unfertilized egg is discharged from the body by a menstrual process that is controlled by the uterus.

Figure 2.3 illustrates the female reproductive system. Notice that the ovaries are glands that lie outside of the reproductive system, although they are an important part of it. The fallopian tubes lead into the uterus. The mouth of the uterus, known as the cervix, leads into the birth canal (vagina).

The Significance of Sexual Intercourse

Internal fertilization is a technique of reproduction that occurs in all vertebrate animals. This simply means that sperm cells must meet egg cells inside the female's body. The process is made possible by copulation or sexual intercourse.

Earlier in this chapter, the effect of sexual arousal of the penis was described. When the penis hardens and becomes erect, it can be inserted in the vagina of the female. The stimulation of copulation triggers a series of contractions that result in ejaculation. The sperm are released within the birth canal and swim through the cervix into the uterus and up to the fallopian tubes. If an egg cell is present, in all probability it will be fertilized.

In humans, the purpose of sexual intercourse is not limited to reproduction. Sexual intercourse provides a necessary emotional release for married or consenting adults. In our society, custom dictates a monogamous way of life; that is, a person may be legally married to only one mate at a time. Supposedly, the concept of one man and one woman forming a marriage unit should regulate sexual practices. It does not. Currently, promiscuity, the use of many sexual partners, seems to be a trend among adults and teenagers. Promiscuity is unhealthy and has led to an increase of venereal disease in epidemic proportions.

Recent reports indicate that sexually active teenagers in the 15-19 age group are becoming infected with sexually transmitted diseases at a rate that can be described as pandemic.

Personal Hygiene and Disease Prevention

The possibility of catching sexually transmitted diseases can be lessened by observing rules of personal hygiene. The microorganisms (germs) that cause venereal diseases are quite sensitive to soap and water. They thrive in the warm, moist, dark environment of the mucous membranes that line the genitals and reproductive organs. Washing the genital area well with soap and water before intercourse and immediately after reduces the number of germs on skin surfaces.

Look carefully at your own body and that of your sex partner. Look for sores, bumps, or redness and observe for foul-smelling discharges. You should avoid sex with a partner who has symptoms of a venereal disease.

Commercial products are on the market that help to reduce the number of disease organisms that enter the body. It is recommended that a condom be worn during sexual intercourse to prevent the spread of germs that cause sexually transmitted diseases.

We believe that young people should not be involved in sexual activities. Sex should be reserved for marriage, and then sexual activities should be engaged in with only one partner.

Some Questions to Think About

1. Why should a young person learn about reproductive systems?
2. Why is internal fertilization important to land animals?
3. Is reproduction necessary to a life or to a species? Explain.
4. List the reasons why engaging in sexual activity is not healthy for junior high school or senior high school students.
5. How can we take care of our reproductive system?
6. Why is care of the reproductive system important?

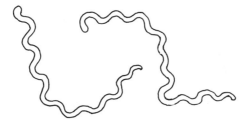

Fig. 3.1. *The spirochete* Treponema pallidum, *which is the causative organism of syphilis.*

scope objective directly. Light is passed through the specimen into the eyepiece.

If a drop of serum containing *T. pallidum* is placed on a slide and examined by dark-field microscopy, the observer can identify the organism by its shape and movement. This treponeme moves backward and forward slowly. It rotates corkscrew-like around the long axis while twisting from side to side.

Syphilis: Two Diseases in One

Syphilis is classified as a communicable disease because it is contagious. Simply stated, this means that one person contracts syphilis from another person who is infected with the disease. Syphilis is classified as a venereal disease because it is transmitted (passed on to another person) only through sexual contact. Specifically, a person becomes infected with the microorganism *T. pallidum* by direct contact with an infectious lesion on the mouth, on the penis, or in the vagina of an infected person.

Figure 3.2 shows an infectious lesion on the mouth of an infected person. An infectious lesion, commonly called a chancre (pronounced shanker), is a pustule or an ulcerated sore that contains spirochetes. How do these spirochetes get from one person to another?

When a healthy person has sexual contact with a person who has syphilis in the infectious stage, spirochetes move onto the skin of the noninfected person. These spirochetes are able to bore through the unbroken mucous membranes that line the genital organs (penis or vagina). Some of the spirochetes remain at the site of infection. Others are carried by the bloodstream to every organ of the body. Within a few hours after exposure to *T. pallidum,* the infection spreads to every organ of the body. We shall now see why syphilis is considered a double disease.

Primary Syphilis

Three weeks after the spirochetes of syphilis enter a new host (infect another person), changes occur in the person's body. The spirochetes that remain at the site of infection begin to reproduce rapidly. Capillaries, hair-like blood vessels, multiply in this area also. Lymph, a clear circulatory fluid, increases at the place where the spirochetes are reproducing. All of this activity results in the formation of a chancre, an infectious lesion filled with spirochetes. This is referred to as a primary lesion of syphilis.

A chancre sore may look terrible. It may be a single or multiple eruption. It may look ulcerated and painful, or it may be hardly more noticeable than a scratch. In most cases, however, regardless of appearance, a chancre is not painful. Sometimes the primary lesion of syphilis is difficult to see. It may be located on the cervix of the vagina, under the foreskin

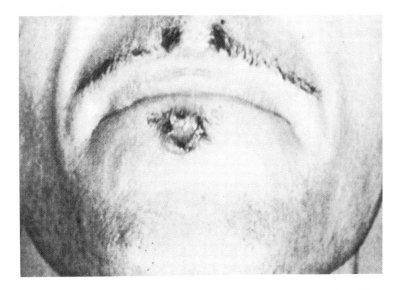

Fig. 3.2. *A chancre is an infectious sore caused by the spirochetes of syphilis.*

of the penis, on the tongue, or within the rectum. It is not unusual for an infected person to be unaware of its presence. If serum (lymph) is taken from the chancre and examined by dark-field microscopy, many of the corkscrew-shaped germs of the species *Treponema pallidum* can be seen.

Within four weeks the primary chancre disappears. The formation of the chancre is the body's attempt to fight off the germs of syphilis. However, the spirochetes do not remain fenced within the chancre. A means of escape is provided by the capillaries that surround the sore. The spirochetes bore into the capillaries and then move into the bloodstream.

Another body defense is the production of antibodies by the body fluids in response to invading organisms. When spirochetes enter the bloodstream, protein molecules known as antibodies are produced. These antibodies are specific for (that is, they will react against) the germs that cause syphilis; but the rate of spirochete reproduction is usually greater than that of antibody production, so the germs are not destroyed. However, the presence of syphilis antibodies in the blood indicates syphilis infection. When a person's blood is tested for syphilis, a positive reaction is one that yields antibodies specific for syphilis.

The primary stage of syphilis is the phase of initial infection. Spirochetes entering the body form a chancre at the site of infection. Ultimately, all of the spirochetes enter the bloodstream and travel to all organs of the body. The chancre disappears.

The Secondary Stage of Syphilis

Because the chancre disappears, some infected persons have a false sense of security and do not seek medical attention. If left untreated, syphilis progresses into a secondary stage, which begins from six weeks to six months after primary infection. By this time, the spirochetes have traveled throughout the body. Untreated, the secondary stage of syphilis may last for as long as two years. The signs of secondary syphilis are unpredictable and varied; however, all the symptoms involve the skin and the mucous membranes that line the body organs. Skin rashes consisting of eruptions of various kinds—raised, flat, spreading, moist, dry—mark the infected person. Figures 3.3 to 3.6 illustrate these. Eruptions appear on the palms of the hands, on the arms, on the body, in the scalp, in the lining of the mouth. Large patches of hair may fall from the scalp and eyebrows. This condition is known as alopecia. Pustules may develop between the toes, in the corners of the mouth, and on the thighs. In addition, the person may have a general feeling of being unwell, suffering from headaches and experiencing low-grade chronic fever, swollen lymph glands, and sore throat. Some people show all of these symptoms; others become aware of one or two of them. These signs of secondary syphilis may last for two or three weeks or may persist for two or more months. During this time, the person is highly infectious and can transmit

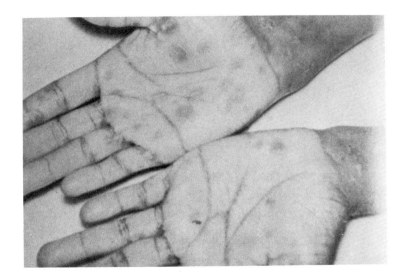

Fig. 3.3. *Pustules of the hand are signs of secondary syphilis.*

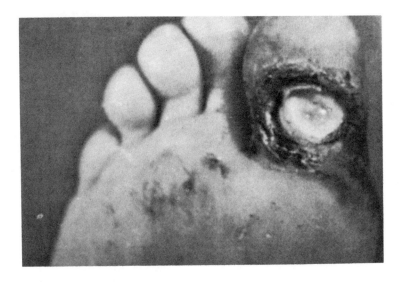

Fig. 3.4. *Ulcer of the toe occurs during late syphilis.*

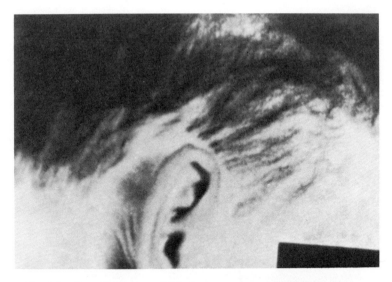

Fig. 3.5. *Alopecia is a loss of hair. It is a symptom of syphilis infection.*

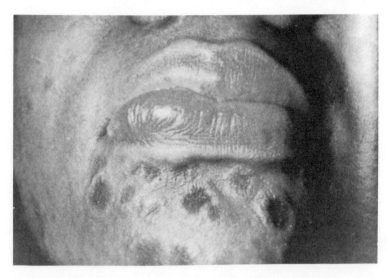

Fig. 3.6. *Facial sores of secondary syphilis. These are known as "nickel and dime" lesions.*

syphilis to another person. In due course, however, the symptoms of secondary syphilis also disappear.

Latent Syphilis

After the disappearance of the symptoms of the secondary stage of syphilis, the disease may remain latent (hidden), with no symptoms. The presence of the disease at this stage can be detected, however, by means of a blood test. Specialists divide the latent stage into two substages: early latent and late latent.

The early latent period represents the phase of infection that is less than four years old; the late latent period is after four years of early latency. At any time within the early latent period, the rashes or other indications of secondary syphilis may recur. During the late latent period, the disease is quiescent.

Syphilis during pregnancy is never quiescent. This topic will be discussed later.

Late Syphilis

The production of antibodies is one of the major body defenses against syphilis. If syphilis remains untreated, the body will ultimately lose the battle. Such is the pattern in one out of every four cases of untreated syphilis. If a person has syphilis for ten years or more, the destruction of body tissues and organs is irreversible; that is, cure is impossible.

One symptom of untreated late syphilis is the gumma. This is a fast-growing large tumor that invades and destroys tissues and organs. Figures 3.7 and 3.8 show gummas of the nose and of the toes. The destructive effect of gummas resembles the disease known as leprosy.

Out of every 100 patients who have latent syphilis, 10 will develop paresis. This is brain damage brought on by the destruction of brain tissue by the spirochetes. The person becomes hopelessly insane.

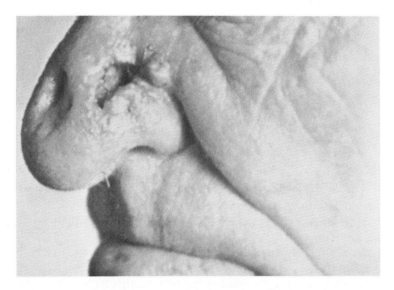

Fig. 3.7. *This tumor of the nose is called a gumma. It is a sign of late syphilis.*

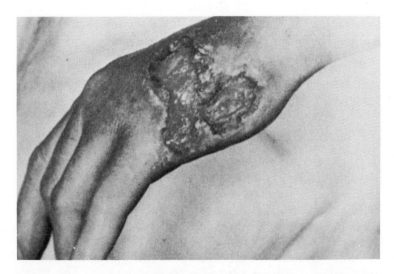

Fig. 3.8. *The tissue-destroying gumma of the hand may occur in a late stage of syphilis.*

Even the neighbors noticed the changes taking place in Mack. As he walked down the street, he would mumble to himself, casting furtive glances over his left shoulder as if he were being followed. At times the mumbling turned into loud raving and scolding at some unseen person. His behavior worsened. He began to carry a wire cutter, which he used to sever perfectly ordinary wires. In his own apartment, he cut the wires to the telephone, toaster, lamps, radio, television, vowing to get rid of "the spies" who were "tuning in" on him. Finally, Mack was removed from his home in a straitjacket. He was incurably insane, suffering from paresis brought on by syphilis.

Another form of nervous system involvement is known as *tabes dorsalis* or locomotor ataxia. Illustrated in Figure 3.9 is the condition known as Charcot knee, which occurs in *tabes dorsalis* of long standing. Not only is there destruction of the knee joint, but also damage to the lower spinal cord. The afflicted person suffers from lightning pains, vomiting, loss of bladder and bowel control, and difficulty in walking.

During late syphilis, another type of damage to the nervous system is also possible. The optic nerve that extends from the brain to the eye can become infected and completely destroyed. Within a week's time a person can become incurably blind.

Out of every 100 people who have late syphilis, 13 are affected with a serious form of heart disease. Spirochetes invade the aorta, the largest artery in the body, and cause the walls of the blood vessel to lose its elasticity. The arterial walls may bubble out, forming what is known as an aneurysm. Sometimes the valves of the heart are damaged by the spirochetes. The person usually dies from coronary insufficiency, meaning that not enough blood is reaching the heart.

Syphilis is considered to be two diseases in one because of the differing symptoms in primary and late syphilis. The signs of primary syphilis are mild, including a chancre that disappears. The symptoms of late syphilis are tissue destruction and are not reversible.

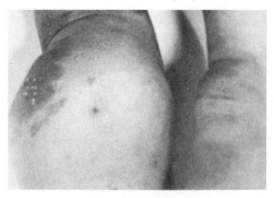

Fig. 3.9. *Charcot knee is caused by damage to the nervous system during late syphilis.*

Syphilis in Pregnancy

Syphilis can be transmitted during an incubation period of 10 to 90 days during the primary stage. It can be transmitted up to the time of skin eruptions during the secondary stage. The patient in the latent and late stages of syphilis is no longer infectious through sexual contact. But the pregnant mother, even in the latent stages, can infect her unborn child, causing death or severe deformities.

Public health officials express concern over the sharp increase in congenital syphilis. (Congenital means present at birth.) In 1980, 300 cases of congenital syphilis were reported; in 1982, 450 cases.

Let us pause for a moment to review facts about human reproduction. The fertilized egg is implanted in the wall of the uterus, which is a thick-walled muscular sac. As the embryo grows in the uterus, several special membranes and organs develop. One of these membranes is the placenta. It connects the embryo to the uterine wall and regulates the exchange of materials between the blood of the mother and the blood of the embryo. The blood systems of the embryo and the mother are separate. However, the capillaries of the mother's blood system and the capillaries from the blood system of the embryo lie close together in the placenta. This permits the diffusion of materials from the mother's blood system into that of the embryo and from the embryo's into that of the mother. It takes nine months for a human embryo to develop into a full-term baby. This time is known as the period of gestation.

Food nutrients, oxygen, antibodies, and other substances diffuse from the mother's blood into the bloodstream of the developing embryo. So do spirochetes of syphilis. Interestingly, the spirochetes do not cross the placenta until after the 18th week of gestation. Prior to this time, an early cell layer in the placenta known as Langhans' layer provides protection against invading spirochetes. As gestation proceeds, Langhan's layer disintegrates, leaving the fetus vulnerable to infection.

If the infected mother is treated before the 18th week of pregnancy, the developing child will not contract syphilis. If the mother remains untreated, the child will be born with congenital syphilis. The descriptions of congenital syphilis that follow are not pleasant. Syphilis is an ugly, deforming, dirty disease, and it may wreak havoc in the newborn.

Congenital syphilis is classified into stages as is acquired syphilis.

Early Congenital Syphilis

The early stage is denoted by symptoms of syphilis that occur before the age of two years. The earlier the onset of syphilis in the young child, the poorer the expectation for the cure or improved health of the child. The symptoms may include:

1. Skin sores. The skin lesions seen in the newborn are encrusted blisters. They are sometimes ulcerated and spreading. They may progress to running sores.
2. Lesions of the mucous membranes. The mucous membrane linings of the nose and throat may be affected by syphilis contagion. A heavy mucous discharge known as the snuffles is produced. At times the newborn baby has heavy nosebleeds. The sores in both the mucous linings and the skin are teeming with spirochetes, causing these lesions to be highly infectious.

3. Anemia, a condition of the blood in which there is a lack of iron. In newborns suffering from syphilis, anemia results from the destruction of red blood cells.
4. Bone involvement. The bones of newborn babies are composed of a great deal of cartilage. As the child develops, calcium is laid down in the bone, resulting in hardening of the long and flat bones. In syphilitic babies, the spirochetes may attack the cartilage of the long bones, causing inflammation and preventing normal deposition of calcium. In some cases the head of the femur, the long bone of the thigh, becomes flattened. The walking child therefore develops a peculiar gait and may be considered crippled.
5. Enlarged spleen and enlarged liver accompanied by jaundice.

Late Congenital Syphilis

Congenital syphilis that has persisted for more than two years is termed late congenital syphilis. The symptoms in this stage may result from continued untreated congenital syphilis or may be the permanent scars or deformities left from previous infection.

1. Eye involvement. The interstitial cells of the cornea of the eye become inflamed. The cells change, and the entire cornea develops a ground-glass appearance. Many capillaries develop in the surrounding portion of the eye known as the sclera. By the time the affected child reaches puberty, blindness in both eyes sets in.
2. Tooth involvement. The spirochetes of syphilis invade the tooth buds in young children, resulting in poorly formed permanent teeth. In many cases the teeth are barrel-shaped, notched, small, and widely spaced. This type of tooth deformity is known as Hutchinson's teeth. In other cases, the molars are poorly developed; instead of having pointed cusps, the molars are rounded. This condition is known as Moon's molars.

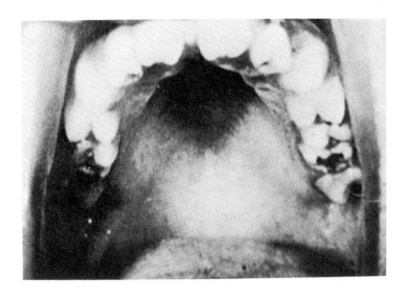

Fig. 3.10. *Hutchinson's teeth is a type of tooth deformity caused when young children are infected with syphilis.*

3. Nervous system involvement. In young people suffering the effects of late congenital syphilis, nervous system involvement can be extensive. Insanity (paresis) is more frequent in children than it is among adults who acquire the disease.
4. Bone involvement. Any part of the skeleton may be involved. The hard palate may fail to develop completely, leaving the structure with a hole in it. The shinbones may become deformed into what is called the saber shin.
5. Other involvement. The skin of the face may be disfigured by syphilitic cracking in infancy. The knee joints may be deformed. Sometimes the heart is malformed.

Treatment

The modern treatment for syphilis is simple, uncomplicated, and effective. In 1943, Dr. John Mahoney, a medical doctor who worked for the United States Public Health Service, was the first to use penicillin in the treatment of syphilis. He used controlled experiments to show that the spirochete of syphilis cannot withstand the effects of this antibiotic.

Fortunately, *Treponema pallidum* has not developed strains that are resistant to penicillin. All forms of syphilis are treated effectively by a single injection of a long-acting penicillin that remains in the blood for two to three weeks. For those persons who are allergic to penicillin, the alternative antibiotics tetracycline and erythromycin are just as effective.

A Word About Diagnosis

Diagnosis refers to those techniques a doctor uses to confirm the presence of a particular disease organism. Because it mimics so many other venereal diseases, syphilis is difficult to diagnose by looking at a person. If a lesion is present, the physician can collect serum from it. If this serum when viewed under a dark-field microscope shows the corkscrew *T. pallidum,* it is almost certain that the patient is infected with syphilis.

Laboratory tests usually confirm the microscopic diagnosis if done about two weeks after the primary lesion develops. The first such test was developed in 1906 by Dr. August von Wasserman and to this day bears his name. In addition to the Wasserman test, other serologic tests are used. These are the Kline, Kahn, Kolmer, and Hinton tests. A serologic test is a blood test in which the serum is examined for antibody formation.

Remember that a test for a disease is not treatment. A test merely tells whether or not a person has the disease. If the test results are positive, the person is considered to have the disease. Treatment is then begun.

The Decline of Syphilis

Since 1962 there has been a steady decline in the number of syphilis cases in New York City. Beginning in that year, the New York City Department of Health waged a massive campaign to educate the public about the symptoms of syphilis. Private physicians were asked to report syphilis cases to the Bureau of Venereal Disease Control. Contacts of infected persons were sought out by trained caseworkers and invited to obtain treatment in free programs in venereal disease centers operated by the Department of Health. Publicity through newsletters, television ads, and radio announcements helped to alert the public to the fact that treatment is available to all who need it.

However, syphilis infection continues to be a health problem among homosexual males. One-half of all cases of syphilis in New York City are in homosexual men. In the rest of the country it is estimated that 35 percent of the syphilis cases are in the male homosexual population. Epidemiologists believe that this figure is not accurate. It probably reflects the fact that, outside of the large cities, male homosexuals do not report their sexual contacts.

The decline in the number of syphilis cases over a period of ten years indicates that proper public health measures reduce the number of cases and improve the health of the community.

However, the number of cases of syphilis has begun to rise again drastically. The spirochete of syphilis has changed (mutated). This new form of the organism is not killed by penicillin, nor are the back-up drugs tetracycline and erythromycin effective against it. Actually, scientists believe that several new strains of the syphilis spirochete are now at work infecting people. Drugs have not yet been developed that are effective against these new strains. A person undergoing treatment for syphilis must have follow-up tests to make sure the treatment is really effective.

It is better to prevent syphilis than to have it cured. Young people are advised to abstain from sexual activity. Everyone is advised to pay serious attention to personal hygiene and adopt the monogamous way of life; that is, to have only one sex partner over a long period of time.

Bureau of Venereal Disease Control to reduce the number of VD cases?

Some Questions to Think About

1. Epidemiology is a study of the ways in which diseases spread. How can epidemiology help to decrease the number of cases of syphilis?
2. Why do Board of Health investigators try to find the sexual contacts of syphilis patients?
3. Why can't modern methods of treatment wipe out syphilis?
4. New York City has been successful in reducing the number of cases of syphilis. What steps must be taken by the Bureau of Venereal Disease Control to reduce the number of VD cases.
5. What has caused the recent increase in the number of cases of syphilis?
6. What advice would you give a friend on ways to avoid syphilis infection?

CHAPTER IV

Gonorrhea, the Ancient Plague of Humans

A Brief History of Gonorrhea

According to medical history, gonorrhea is the oldest of the venereal diseases. As far back as 2637 B.C. it was known to the ancient Chinese. The Emperor Huang-ti proclaimed that the reproductive system of women gave off a fluid that caused the disease in men. The ancient Hebrews tried to control the spread of gonorrhea by enacting sanitary laws. The Greek philosopher Hippocrates described its symptoms, and the Greek physician Galen (130 A.D.) named the disease gonorrhea.

During the fifteenth century gonorrhea raged throughout Europe. The infected crew of Columbus' ships brought the disease to America and gave it to the Indian women. In return, they were infected with syphilis. In those days it was not uncommon for people to have both diseases at the same time. Thus the sixteenth-century physicians thought that gonorrhea was the beginning stage of syphilis, and this false idea persisted for over 300 years.

To Philippe Ricord (1800–89) goes the credit for determining that gonorrhea and syphilis are two separate diseases. Ricord, born in the U.S. of French parentage, was a first-rate investigator. He studied more than 2,500 human discharges and in 1838 was able to prove without doubt that gonorrhea and syphilis are not related. Albert Neisser (1855–1916), a German doctor, in 1879 discovered the organism that causes gonorrhea.

What Causes Gonorrhea?

Gonorrhea is an infectious disease caused by the gonococcus bacterium. A round bacterium is known as a coccus (pl., cocci). The prefix *gono* comes from a Greek word meaning seed or egg. Therefore, the word gonococcus aptly describes the parasite that causes this disease. *Neisseria gonorrhoeae* is the scientific name given the bacterium, in recognition of its discoverer.

The bacteria of gonorrhea appear in pairs and cannot live outside of the body. In fact this parasite lives only on a particular type of tissue. We have seen that tissues are composed of cells. Columnar epithelial cells make up the kind of tissue that covers certain parts of the body, including the lining of the mouth, the rectum, the eyelids, the sperm tubes of men, and the cervix of women. Something in these tissue cells provides nourishment for *N. gonorrhoeae.*

It is not true that a person can become infected with gonorrhea by touching a contaminated doorknob or sitting on a public toilet seat. Neither is it possible for a person to become infected with the disease because of breaks in the skin. Gonococcus parasites are fragile. They die on exposure to air for even a short time. They cannot live on the tissues of other animals. They must have fluids produced by the columnar epithelial cells, and they must have a constant body temperature. These bacteria cannot move around. The only way in which gonorrhea spreads is by sexual intercourse. An infected person passes the bacteria to a victim of the opposite sex or the same sex. There is one exception to this rule. Gonorrhea in newborns is contracted in a different way. This is discussed later in the chapter.

How Does Gonorrhea Affect Males?

Let us suppose that a healthy male has sexual intercourse with a female who has gonorrhea. The gonococcus bacteria pass from the vagina of the female into the urethra of the male. In the new location the tissue cells, the body fluids, and the temperature favor the rapid reproduction of the bacteria. Every ten or fifteen minutes each bacterium goes through a cell division in which it becomes two. Simple mathematics

will tell you that in a very short time there will be thousands
of these organisms.

When foreign bacteria invade human tissue, the body's defenses become activated. White blood cells rush to the site of
infection to devour the bacteria. But there are so many bacteria that the white blood cells are killed. Dead white blood
cells and dead bacteria form pus. The time during which the
bacteria are reproducing is called the *incubation period.* It
can range from two days to three weeks after infectious sexual
contact.

Known popularly as "the clap," "a dose," "G.C.," or "the
drip," gonorrhea is a serious venereal disease. After the incubation period in infected males, symptoms of the disease
begin to appear. A burning sensation, frequency of urination,
and a discharge of pus from the penis indicate that something
is wrong. These symptoms are usually so disturbing that the
victim seeks medical help. At this stage, the gonococci are
localized in the urethra.   *91-17806*

If the primary infection remains untreated, more serious
developments take place. Traveling up the urethra, the gonococci spread into the prostate gland, which is located at the
base of the bladder. They move also into the seminal vesicles,
the epididymis, Cowper's gland, and the vas deferens; see
Figure 2.1 to locate these organs. Remember that the gonococci destroy tissue. When tissue is destroyed and healed over,
scar tissue forms. Scar tissue is not like other tissue; it is less
flexible, less elastic, and thicker. A number of small coiled
tubules are contained in the testes, through which sperm pass.
If the tubules are blocked by scar tissue, however, the passage
of sperm is blocked. The inability to pass sperm makes a male
sterile. This is a consequence of untreated gonorrhea. Prior to
sterility, painful abscesses may drain through the urethra or
rectum. It is quite possible for the bacteria of gonorrhea to be
carried by the bloodstream and spread to the joints and
spaces between the joints, causing gonococcal arthritis. In a
few cases, the disease may affect the heart, blood vessels, and
brain.

How Does Gonorrhea Affect Females?

Now let us suppose that an infected male passes the *Neisseria gonorrhoeae* to a female victim. The usual primary site of infection for the female is the cervix. This organ lies deep in the reproductive tract and therefore masks the symptoms of gonorrhea infection.

Gonorrhea in the female presents a varied picture. Sometimes there may be mild urinary discomfort, mild burning, or urination frequency. There may be a light puslike discharge from the vagina. Usually, however, the symptoms are so mild that little attention is paid to them. In some females there are no symptoms of infection. In either case, left untreated the disease moves into the acute stage.

When the bacteria migrate to other organs of the reproductive system, the acute stage of infection begins. Avoiding the uterus, the gonococci settle in the fallopian tubes and the ovaries. A great deal of pus forms and spills over into the abdomen, causing inflammation. Pelvic pain and high fever may result. In some cases the pain and fever are severe; in other cases, mild. Sometimes the pain of gonorrhea resembles that of appendicitis. Abscesses may form and drain through the vagina or rectum.

If the acute stage is left untreated, chronic infection occurs. The tissues of the fallopian tubes and ovaries may be destroyed by the bacteria. The formation of scar tissue in the fallopian tubes may render the female sterile. More serious, however, is the possibility that large tubo-ovarian abscesses may rupture. Toxins discharged into the abdominal cavity can cause rapid shock and death. In some females, as in males, chronic gonorrhea may result in arthritis and heart disease.

Gonorrhea in the pregnant woman has very serious effects. As was stated before, gonococcus bacteria live only on certain tissue. Columnar epithelial tissue not only covers the organs of the reproductive system, but also lines the eyelids and covers the eyeballs of the newborn. If a pregnant woman has gonorrhea, the bacteria that cause the disease are present in the cervix and in the birth canal. As the baby is being born, it passes through the birth canal and thus through the area of infection. The gonococci pass from the infected mother into the eyes of the newborn.

Within a very short time after delivery, symptoms of infection appear in the baby's eyes. The cornea becomes severely inflamed. Pus is discharged from the eyes. The corneal covering of the eyeball is destroyed, and scar tissue results. The damage to the eyes renders the baby blind for life. In order to prevent tragedy of this kind, most states have enacted laws requiring attending physicians to put drops of silver nitrate or antibiotic into the child's eyes immediately on birth. This prevents infection by *N. gonorrhoeae.*

Fig. 4.1. *PPGN can appear in any community.*

How Is Gonorrhea Diagnosed and Treated?

One of the best methods available to the doctor for diagnosing a disease depends on laboratory work. The doctor obtains a sample of the suspected disease-causing organism from the patient's body. In the case of gonorrhea in the male, the doctor takes a sample of the discharge from the urethra and looks for the gonococci in this discharge. In women, samples of fluid have to be taken from the cervix. The specimen is specially cultured and stained with a fluorescent dye. The stained gonococci are viewed under ultraviolet light.

Gonorrhea is best treated with a single large dose of an injectable short-acting penicillin. Gonococci respond to a high blood level of penicillin. However, some strains of the organism have become resistant to penicillin.

Penicillin-Resistant Gonorrhea

In March 1976, the Federal Center for Disease Control in Atlanta, Georgia, identified the first case of penicillin-resistant gonorrhea to be recorded in the United States. "Penicillin-resistant" means that the germ that causes the gonorrhea is not destroyed by penicillin, but lives rather well in an environment where there is penicillin. Therefore, gonorrhea that is caused by a penicillin-resistant germ cannot be cured by the usual treatment with the antibiotic penicillin.

As you know, gonorrhea is caused by the bacterium *Neisseria gonorrhoeae*. The bacterium that is responsible for penicillin-resistant gonorrhea is known as *Penicillinase-producing Neisseria gonorrhoeae*. Since this is a complicated name, scientists have shortened it to PPNG. Note the ending of the word penicillin*ase*. The "ase" ending tells us that this substance is an enzyme. Enzymes are chemical substances, manufactured by cells in the digestive system, that speed up digestion. Therefore, penicillinase is an enzyme that is able to break down or digest penicillin. Once penicillin is broken down, it is no longer useful as a medication against *N. gonorrhoeae*.

The events that led to the emergence of the penicillin-resistant strain of *N. gonorrhoeae* are worth telling as an example of the way in which humans can unwittingly invite the growth of mutant (changed) forms of bacteria. Penicillin is used universally to cure gonorrhea. It came to be misused in the Philippines and some countries of the Far East. Instead of using the antibiotic to cure gonorrhea, people began to use it as a preventive medication against the disease. Prostitutes and other persons with abnormally active sex lives took penicillin capsules regularly to prevent the contracting of gonorrhea. What actually happened was this. The number of the usual strain of *N. gonorrhoeae* was greatly reduced by the frequent doses of penicillin. Doing away with the normal strain of the gonorrhea organism removed competition for the growth of a mutant (gene-changed) strain. This new type of organism is not affected by penicillin and can grow in body tissues even though the antibiotic is present.

To date, 4,763 cases of penicillin-resistant gonorrhea have been reported in the fifty states, the District of Columbia, and Guam. Penicillin-resistant has become epidemic.

Treating PPNG

The increase in PPNG has very serious effects on the health of a community. Penicillin is a rather inexpensive, readily available antibiotic that cures gonorrhea infection. When this medication is no longer useful in treatment of gonorrhea, another means of therapy has to be used. Thus PPNG is a very serious threat to the control of VD in large cities.

The increase in the cost of treating persons with gonorrhea is enormous. Before treatment can be started, doctors must find out if the gonorrhea organisms infecting the patient are of the resistant type. This can be done only by expensive laboratory tests. If the organisms produce the specific enzyme called Beta-Lactamase, they are penicillin-resistant. At present, two relatively new medications are tried: spectinomycin and cefoxitan. When spectinomycin fails to clear up an infection, cefoxitan is used. These treatments must be given daily for five to ten days. Doctors must follow up the patients regularly to check on return of the disease.

Pelvic Inflammatory Disease

Pelvic inflammatory disease (PID) is an infection that extends from the cervix up into the fallopian tubes. The infection is caused by various microorganisms that enter the body through sexual contact. Pelvic inflammatory disease is the most frequently occurring complication of gonorrhea. It is believed that more than 17 percent of women who have untreated gonorrhea develop PID. If this percentage is rendered in numbers, 240,000 women in the United States develop PID annually as the result of gonorrhea. In a large number of cases of PID, the patient seems not to harbor the gonococcus; therefore, the total number of cases of PID that occur each year in the U.S. may be as high as 550,000.

Pelvic inflammatory disease is destructive. It may expose the infected female to serious long-term complications, including repeated infections, continuing pain in the pelvic region, ectopic (tube) pregnancy, and sterility. *Neisseria gonorrheae* is generally considered the most common cause of PID. Therefore, PID is divided into gonococcal and nongonococcal forms, depending on whether or not *N. gonorrheae* is found in the discharge from the cervix. It is not unusual for the gonorrhea organism not to be found in patients suffering from PID. Doctors believe that the gonococci may be responsible for beginning the infection and then paving the way for secondary infectious microorganisms.

It has been found that anaerobic bacteria may be the infecting organisms in nongonococcal PID. An anaerobic bacterium is one that lives in places where there is little oxygen. The types of bacteria that have been isolated in PID cultures are *Bacteroides fragilis,* peptostreptococci, and peptococci. About eight other kinds of bacteria have been found in discharges from PID patients. This means that PID is a serious and complicated infection caused by a host of infecting bacteria.

The route of infection in gonococcal PID is most interesting. It is believed that gonococci are transported to the fallopian tubes by sperm cells. Gonococci are able to attach themselves to human sperm by means of their hairlike pili. The bacteria are then carried by the swimming sperm. The progress of PID infections seems to be speeded by menstruation. Menstruation lowers the body's resistance to organisms that can cause infection of the reproductive tract. The invasion of bacteria is helped by the sloughing off of the endometrium and the presence of blood during the menses. Some of the endometrial blood may pass backward into the fallopian tubes, carrying with it infectious organisms.

When infectious bacteria enter the fallopian tubes, they attach themselves to the epithelial cells that line these tubes. Phagocytes (white blood cells) surround and destroy them. The epithelial cells are also destroyed. All of these events lead to the formation of pus in the tubes. The pus may infect underlying tissues and eventually fill the peritoneal cavity. Inflammation of the ovaries and the bowel may result. Nongonococcal PID is caused by a host of invading bacteria. The route that they travel through the body is the same as that of the gonococcal form, and they cause the same destruction of tissue.

The occurrence of PID has been associated quite closely with the use of the intrauterine device (IUD) for birth control. It has been estimated that the risk of acquiring PID is three times as great in IUD users as in those who do not use the device. In women who have never been pregnant, the corresponding risk factor is seven times as great. Most of the serious PID infections take place after the IUD has been in place for a long period of time. It is known that an IUD can change the cell structure of the endometrium, causing the wearing away of cells in the walls of the uterus. The areas from which cells have been eroded often become infected with microorganisms that travel into the uterus. The infection moves upward to the fallopian tubes and often into the ovaries.

The signs of PID are fever, chills, listlessness, loss of appetite, nausea, indigestion, vomiting, and abdominal pain. The pain may be mild and passed off as cramps. In some women the pain is so severe that it prevents them from carrying out normal daily activities. Other symptoms of PID are vaginal discharge, pain when urinating, and other forms of distress related to the urinary or intestinal tract.

Treatment of PID is by large doses of penicillin or tetracycline. The patient should be under daily observation and should be checked frequently for the appearance of the gonococcus organism. Pelvic inflammatory disease is serious. Although it rarely leads to death, it makes a person ill over a long span of time if not treated.

Summary

Neisseria gonorrhoeae is the causative organism of gonorrhea. Untreated gonorrhea can lead to sterility in both males and females. Under normal circumstances, gonorrhea can be cured by penicillin injections. A new strain of gonorrhea called PPNG has appeared. Penicillin has no effect on this strain, and therefore gonorrhea caused by this germ has become epidemic. New laboratory methods and treatments are now being used in an effort to control PPNG.

Some Questions to Think About

1. Which disease is found more frequently in a population, gonorrhea or syphilis?
2. What are the dangers of untreated gonorrhea?
3. How might the incidence of gonorrhea be reduced in a population?
4. Why is patient follow-up important in the control of PPNG?
5. Why should persons infected with gonorrhea give the names of recent sexual contacts to the health investigative teams?
6. Why has the appearance of PPNG increased the cost of treatment of gonorrhea patients?

CHAPTER V

Venereal Herpes:
The Hide and Creep Disease

You know that infectious diseases are caused by organisms that enter the body and do harm to its tissues. Organisms too small to be detected by the naked eye but large enough to be seen through the light microscope are called *microorganisms*. The spirochete of syphilis, *Treponema pallidum,* and the round bacterium that causes gonorrhea, *Neisseria gonorrhoeae,* are examples of disease-producing microorganisms, or *pathogens*. In everyday language, pathogens are referred to as germs. Germs that enter the body by way of the genital organs produce diseases that are called venereal diseases. Modern physicians refer to the venereal diseases as *sexually transmitted diseases,* abbreviated STD.

Cell Division of Germs

The body of a germ usually consists of a single cell. Structures within the cell body enable it to carry out biochemical activities necessary for its life. Each cell is surrounded by a plasma membrane specialized to control the passage of materials into and out of the cell body. Just inside of the plasma membrane is the cytoplasm, where the work of the cell is accomplished. The nucleus, with its chromosomes and DNA molecules, directs reproduction. When germ cells mature and reach a certain size, they go through the process of cell division, in which two new cells are produced from a single parent. Cell division is an orderly series of events involving each cell's own chromosomes, DNA molecules, and cytoplasm. Although bacteria do not have an organized nucleus, they do have a circular chromosome, composed of DNA molecules, which behaves much like the chromosomes in other

germ cells and directs the process of reproduction. Under
favorable conditions, bacteria may reproduce every fifteen
minutes. The rates at which other microorganisms reproduce
vary.

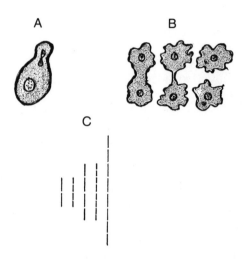

Fig. 5.1. *Some one-celled organisms: (A) budding yeast cell;
(B) binary fission in bacteria; (C) dividing amoeba.*

The Virus: A Biological Puzzle

Venereal and nonvenereal diseases are caused by germs of
various species: spirochetes, bacteria, yeasts, molds, and protozoa. All of these are *living* single-celled organisms. Another
large and important group of disease producers are the
viruses.

Viruses are particles too small to be seen either by the
naked eye or by the light microscope. Some virus particles are
large enough to be photographed by the electron microscope,
a device able to magnify a specimen more than 200,000 times.
Because of its small size, a virus is measured in light units
called *nanometers.* A nanometer is equivalent to 8 millionths
of an inch. Viruses range in size from 17 to 300 nanometers.

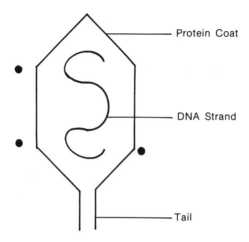

Fig. 5.2. *Structure of a virus.*

A free, unattached virus is known as a *virion*. Its structure consists of a protein coat or *capsid* and either a single or double strand of a nucleic acid. Some virus particles contain the nucleic acid DNA, deoxyribonucleic acid. Other viruses contain RNA, ribonucleic acid. A few viruses, such as those that cause influenza and CMV infection, are wrapped in a plasma membrane that comes from the living cell in which the virus reproduces. Later we shall see how the virus gets a coat of plasma membrane from a living cell.

Scientists are puzzled by viruses because these particles do not look like or behave like living cells. You know that all living cells carry out certain biochemical life functions such as ingestion, or the taking in of food; digestion, in which large molecules are reduced to small-sized nutrients; excretion, to get rid of wastes; and reproduction, in which the cell makes more of its kind.

Biologists classify the virus as a nonliving particle because it does not carry on any of the life functions except reproduction. Viruses are biologically inactive and seemingly nonliving. They neither take in food nor use it for respiration, and they

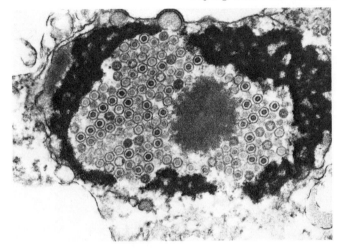

Fig. 5.3. *Cell invaded by herpes simplex virus (courtesy Burroughs Wellcome Co.).*

"come alive" only when inside of living cells. Not until a virus gets inside a living cell can it reproduce itself. *Replication* is the name given to the special method of viral reproduction.

A virus cannot enter any type of cell. The host cell must have a special place on the plasma membrane (receptor site) to which the virus can attach itself. The virus, too, has a place on its coat that matches the receptor site of its host. Once attachment takes place, either of two events may occur. The virus may shed its protein coat, and then the nucleic acid strand (DNA or RNA) of the virus is injected into the host cell. Or the virus may not shed its coat after attachment to the host cell; rather, the entire virus particle, coat and DNA, enters the cell. When the intact virus enters a cell, the protein coat is destroyed by enzymes. In either case, once invaded by the nucleic acid of a virus, a living cell is taken over completely by the virus. Using the materials of the host cell, the virus is able to reproduce itself. So great a number of viruses are replicated within one cell that the cell bursts open, releasing the newly formed virus particles into the body fluids. These new virions invade other cells until the immune system of the body is called into action and prevents further raids on the body cells.

Like other pathogens, viruses enter the body through the nose, mouth, or skin. Once inside the body, disease-producing viruses invade specific cells, and the infected person becomes ill. You have read about diseases such as chicken pox, mumps, measles, smallpox, yellow fever, influenza, viral pneumonia, and the common cold. All of these diseases are caused by viruses.

The Herpesvirus Group

Although virus particles are not units of living matter, each virus group behaves differently inside the body. Viruses are classified by the kinds of diseases they produce. They are known by their mode of action in the body. Herpes is the name given to a group of viruses that cause a great many human illnesses.

Taken from the Greek word meaning "to creep," the name herpes describes a group of viruses that are able to hide in the body for indefinite periods of time without causing harm. Then, seemingly without warning, they creep out of hiding and cause distress. Herpes-produced illnesses range from mild skin eruptions and fever to serious tissue and organ damage. Interestingly, some types of herpesviruses do not infect humans but are specific for the cells of particular animal species: chickens, oysters, turkeys, and frogs. Our concern in this chapter will be for those herpesvirus types that infect humans by way of venereal pathways.

Because the herpesvirus can reproduce itself only within living cells, it is known as an obligate intracellular (within cells) parasite. The herpes parasites kill most of the cells they invade by using the cells' DNA to make more virus particles. The host cell is destroyed as hundreds of virus particles burst through their nuclear and plasma membranes. (Some viruses, such as the influenza virus, become permanently wrapped in membranes torn from their host cells. The effect of these membranes on the virus particle is not known.)

To date, six herpesvirus types have been identified. According to Dr. Clyde Crumpacker of Harvard Medical School and Beth Israel Hospital in Boston, these six types of herpesviruses probably cause more human illness than any other virus group. The accompanying table presents a summary of the six herpes-type viruses that cause human illness.

HERPES TYPE VIRUSES

Virus Name	Abbreviation	Illness Caused
Varicella-zoster	VZ	chicken pox
Herpes-zoster	HZ	shingles in adults
Epstein-Barr virus	EBV	infectious mononucleosis
Cytomegalovirus	CMV	severe infant infection recurrent adult illnesses
Herpes simplex virus type 1	HSV-1	nonvenereal cold sores and fever blisters
Herpes simplex virus type 2	HSV-2	genital herpes

Herpes Simplex Virus

There are two strains of the herpes simplex virus, identified as type 1 and type 2. Both strains cause cold sores and fever blisters and are passed from one person to another by contact. Herpes simplex virus type 1 (HSV-1) is nonvenereal, whereas HSV-2 is venereal, passing from one person to another by way of the genital organs.

According to current information, children may become infected with HSV-1 before puberty. The infection is passed from an adult with whom the child has close contact. The child may be kissed or touched by the adult, who is shedding (giving off) virus from an active cold sore. The virus enters the child's body, boring through the skin around the lips or through the mucous membranes in the mouth. The virus does not need broken skin to enter the body.

An important characteristic of herpesvirus is that it can hide in the body, remaining dormant (quiet) for months or even years. After entering the body, it travels along sensory nerve pathways in the face. The virus hides in the ganglia of the sensory (trigeminal) nerve, which passes along the cheek and extends to the base of the brain.

How long HSV-1 remains dormant depends upon the general condition of a person's health and well-being. For reasons not yet understood, the virus can be activated by body changes such as exposure to sun, illness, fever, stress, and allergy brought on by foods, emotional upset, or any drug or disease that supresses the body's immune response. The awakened HSV-1 travels down the trigeminal nerve back to the site of infection. It invades cells, replicates, and forms the fluid-filled sores known as fever blisters near the lips or in the mouth.

The sores of herpes last about two or three weeks and then gradually decrease in size. As the fluid dries up, the skin around the sore begins to heal. When healing takes place, the virus particles travel up the sensory nerve pathway and again remain dormant among the ganglia until awakened once more. A disease that comes back is known as a *recurrent disorder*. Herpes infections are recurrent. Those infected with herpes cannot predict when the symptoms will return. It is believed that herpes outbreaks signal low body resistance, which may be brought on by stress or weakened general health. Fever blisters are not the only symptoms of herpes infection. Some people experience fever, aching joints, tiredness, and a generally unwell feeling.

Genital Herpes

Herpes simplex virus type 2 is transmitted by sexual intercourse. Like other herpes, HSV-2 does not need broken skin to enter the body, but can penetrate the mucous membranes of the genital organs. Sores appear at the site of infection, which may be the penis, vagina, anus, buttocks, or thighs. Herpes simplex virus-2 may also cause sores on the lips or in the mouth as a consequence of oral sex. Between two and twenty days after infection, the symptoms of genital herpes appear. The symptoms are most severe during the first infection. At the onset they may include burning, itching, or numbness, followed by headache and fever, muscle ache, and swollen glands. Over a period of ten days, the symptoms worsen, and painful sores appear. The eruption may be a single sore or a cluster of oozing sores. Genital herpes in women may cause a burning sensation during urination and may also stimulate vaginal discharge.

The virus of genital herpes hides in the body. It tracks along the sacral ganglion, a nerve pathway located just outside of the spinal cord. When the HSV-2 is activated, it travels down the sacral pathway to the original site of infection, bringing about the formation of genital sores, poor appetite, and an overall feeling of being unwell.

Genital Herpes, a Serious Health Problem

Genital herpes is fast becoming a major health problem, affecting one in five American adults. Dr. Fred Rapp, microbiologist at Hersey Medical School and a leading herpes research worker, expresses concern that there may be 30 million infected persons in the near future. It is estimated that HSV-1 has infected from 50 million to 150 million persons.

Genital herpes has recurrent symptoms. Once HSV-2 gets into the body, *it does not leave.* There is strong evidence that cells infected by HSV-2 can turn into cancer cells.

Cancer of the cervix (the neck of the uterus) occurs much too frequently in the female population. Cancer cells taken from women suffering from cervical cancer have revealed some amazing and alarming information. Pieces of DNA molecules belonging to DNA genital herpesviruses have been found in human cancer cells. Another worrying fact is that women married to men whose first wives had cervical cancer are very likely to contract cervical cancer also. It may be that the husband, herpes infected, transmits the virus to the wife. Based on experimental evidence, it can be assumed that HSV-2 can change normal cervix cells into abnormal cancer cells.

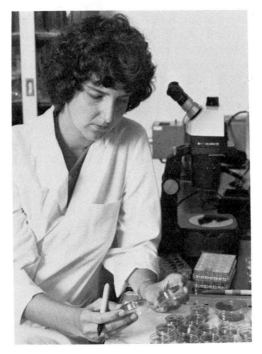

Fig. 5.4. *A technician counts plaque on a herpes virus-infected cell culture (courtesy Burroughs Wellcome Co.).*

Genital Herpes, a Disease for Life

Any disease-bearing cell or particle that canot be removed from the body causes a serious threat to health. Once the herpesvirus enters the body, it remains there for life. Venereal diseases such as syphilis and non-penicillin-resistant gonor-rhea can be treated and cured by antibiotics, but herpesvirus is not affected by antibiotics. (A drug is now available that is somewhat effective against cold sores; more will be said about it later in the chapter.) In fact, there is no known cure for herpes infection. A person with genital herpes has the disease for life.

Herpes, the "virus of love," affects both physical well-being
and mental health. The fact that the infection is permanent
means that a person is never free of its effects. The recurrence
of the disease works a mental hardship on the infected person,
who has always to worry about impending flareups. Some
people suffer great physical discomfort from the active infection; others, hardly at all. Those severely affected may experience eruptions of sores and other symptoms nine to twelve
times a year. Just before the blisters appear, the muscles may
ache or experience tingling sensations. Body responses that
signal the recurrence of herpes infection are called *prodomes.*
Not all persons infected by the herpesvirus experience prodomes. Without the warning, a person in quiet and guilt-
ridden depression awaits the next outbreak of the disease.

Another serious consequence of herpes infection is that a
man or woman who is so infected is a disease carrier for the
rest of his or her life. In some herpes carriers the symptoms of
the disease are very mild and may be practically nonexistent.
However, at certain intervals these silent carriers, as they are
called, actively shed the virus, passing it on to unsuspecting
sex partners.

Herpes carriers suffer a great deal of mental anguish,
referred to by psychologists as the "herpes syndrome." A syndrome is a set of emotions or feelings that form an identifiable
pattern. The pattern of emotions expressed by herpes victims
reflects deep despair ranging from feelings of uncleanliness to
burning rage to morbid fear. It is not unusual for herpes
sufferers to retreat to a life of social isolation, giving up
friends and turned inward. Support groups have been formed
that help herpetics overcome the feeling of guilt and social
isolation.

Acyclovir, a Medical Breakthrough

You recall that the herpesvirus, like other viral particles,
can reproduce only within living cells. The cells selected by
the herpesvirus for invasion are those that have viral recognition sites on their cell membranes. Once the virus enters the

cell, it uses the cell's DNA to make more virus particles. In order to make viral DNA, the herpesvirus carries the enzymes necessary to produce three kinds of virus proteins. If one of these enzymes is made inactive, herpesvirus DNA cannot be produced and virus replication cannot take place.

Acyclovir is an antiviral drug effective against herpesviruses. Acyclovir has the ability to prevent the synthesis of DNA polymerase, one of the three enzymes necessary for the production of virus DNA. When the synthesis of DNA polymerase is blocked, the herpesvirus cannot replicate.

Acyclovir is a white, crystalline powder that is incorporated into an ointment sold under the brand name Zovirax. This medication is used externally only, applied to the blisters caused by HSV-1 or HSV-2. The effect of Zovirax is to shorten the time that the sores are present on the lips or the genitalia. Fluid-filled herpes sores contain active viruses. Zovirax prevents the replication of the viruses in the sores and therefore reduces the time of viral shedding. In addition, the ointment eases the pain that accompanies the blisters.

Acyclovir is not a cure for herpesvirus. It cannot prevent the transmission of the disease from carrier to victim. The medication merely reduces the symptoms of herpesvirus infection: it shortens the duration of cold sores, reduces the amount of viral shedding, and decreases pain.

Acyclovir in tablet form to be taken orally is currently being tested. Dr. Yvonne J. Bryson, who heads the research team at the UCLA School of Medicine, reported that patients who took acyclovir orally for only forty-eight hours had no new outbreaks of infectious sores, but they occurred for up to ten days in patients not receiving the drug. Because the sores shed the virus, eliminating the virus very fast reduces the chance of passing it on. Oral acyclovir is expected to be approved for the commercial market by the U.S. FDA.

Another form of Zovirax for intravenous (through the veins) use is being tested. It is intended for treatment of patients whose herpes infection is so severe that they must be hospitalized. It should be noted that all forms of acyclovir are used only for initial attacks of genital herpes.

Other Drugs Under Investigation

An antiherpes drug called Biolf-62 has been synthesized at McGill University, Montreal, Canada, and is being tested on animals at the University of Texas. Biolf-62 seems to be effective against a large number of herpes strains and to have fewer side effects than other treatments. The drug has not yet been tested on humans.

Two other drugs for use with genital herpes are being tested on laboratory animals. One of the drugs, ABPP, is designed to prevent infection; the other, cyclaradine, is to be used for treatment after infection has occurred. Neither drug has yet been approved for human testing.

Summary

Genital herpes is caused by infection by herpes simplex virus type 2. HSV-2 is transmitted from carrier to victim by means of sexual intercourse. The virus bores through the unbroken mucous membranes of the genitals and hides in the ganglia of certain sensory nerves. Triggered by body conditions such as stress, low resistance, illness, or excessive exposure to sun, the herpesvirus becomes activated, forming painful sores at the site of infection. There is no cure for herpes infection; the virus remains in a person's body for life. Zovirax ointment reduces the duration and pain of the blisters, but does not cure the disease.

Some Questions to Think About

1. In what important way is genital herpes different from syphilis and gonorrhea?
2. What is the relationship between genital herpes and cancer?
3. How does herpes simplex virus type 2 reproduce?
4. What factors may trigger the recurrence of genital herpes?
5. List the reasons why genital herpes is considered to be a major health problem.

CHAPTER VI

Cytomegalovirus, the Baby Destroyer

There is a branch of medical science that deals with identifying and charting the kinds of diseases that appear among people in the various regions of the world. The science of "keeping tabs" on the spread of disease is called *epidemiology*. If you look carefully at this word, you will see that it is closely related to the word *epidemic*. An epidemic is an uncontrolled spread of a disease. Epidemiology is the science that charts the spread of all diseases. The scientist who does this work is called an *epidemiologist*.

The work of the epidemiologist is very important. Through statistical studies of disease distribution and rates of disease appearance, the general health of a nation can be assessed. Epidemiology not only tells us about the kinds of diseases that are infecting human beings, but also the speed at which these infections are moving from one geographical area to another. Based on information gathered by epidemiologists, local boards of health plan programs to protect the health of the people in their communities.

Cytomegalovirus Infection

According to the most recent epidemiology reports, between 30,000 and 40,000 infants in the United States are born annually with cytomegalovirus (CMV) infection, and the number increases each year. Many infants acquire CMV infection before birth and are said to have a *congenital* infection. A *perinatal* infection is one that is acquired at the time of delivery. Infection acquired later in life is known as *postnatal* infection. The terms congenital, perinatal, and postnatal are important only in so far as they help us understand the nature of a particular body disorder.

You read in Chapter V that six types of herpesviruses infect human beings. We have already discussed genital herpes, and you know how this virus enters the body, how serious are its effects on a person's health. Just like HSV-2, cytomegalovirus may enter the body through venereal pathways and may be spread from one person to another during sexual contact. Scientists tell us that not all CMV infections are spread venereally; however, to get the infection one must have very close contact with a person who is shedding the virus.

Virion Structure

The virus of cytomegalovirus infection looks very much like the virus of herpes simplex. Its protein coat is surrounded by living membrane. Since cytomegalovirus is a DNA virus, it replicates in the nucleus of a living cell, producing hundreds of identical virus particles. As these CMV particles burst out of the nuclei of the invaded epithelial cells, some of the cell's nuclear membrane remains attached to each virus. The effect of the membrane coat on the virus is not known. CMV not only reproduces inside of epithelial cells, but also invades white blood cells.

This virus is about 250 nanometers in diameter and can be photographed quite well through an electron microscope. Strangely, CMV is so fragile that it is readily destroyed by acid pH, heat, and freezing then thawing. It is remarkable that so delicate a virus can infect so large a part of the population.

Distribution of CMV

Cytomegalovirus infections are widely distributed throughout the world. In countries where health practices are primitive, 80 to 90 percent of the population becomes infected with this virus during early childhood. In the United States and other health-concerned countries, the rate of infection is slower. Infection by CMV usually occurs at puberty or shortly thereafter. If this virus is so widespread, why is it that infection is not seen in 85 percent of the population? Like others of the herpesviruses, CMV is able to hide in the body, remaining dormant for long periods of time. In a great percentage of the population, CMV infection is *asymptomatic*, that is, the signs of infection are extremely mild or nonexistent. However, even those persons who are not actively ill from the infection actively shed the virus at various intervals.

Postnatal infection takes place sometime between puberty and early adulthood, and may well be of nonvenereal origin. Symptoms of CMV infection resemble those of infectious mononucleosis, which is caused by the Epstein-Barr virus. Fever, headache, and back and abdominal pain are the major symptoms of CMV infection in adults. Sometimes these symptoms are accompanied by a fine rash, inflammation of the eye, hemorrhaging under the skin, and inflammation of the nerve endings in the face. In extreme cases, results of CMV infection may be inflammation of the membranes of the heart, inflammation of the heart muscles, or hemolytic anemia in which there is bursting of the red blood cells.

Cytomegalovirus Infection in Infants

Cytomegalovirus infection may occur at any of three stages in an infant's life. Before birth, the fetus may become infected when cells in the mother's uterus harbor virus. Penetrating the delicate fetal tissues, CMV viruses invade the epithelial linings and the white blood cells of the unborn. If the cells of the mother's cervix are infected with CMV virus, the infant can be infected as it passes through the birth canal. CMV virus may be transmitted to the newborn by infected milk. It is not unusual for pregnant mothers to have asymptomatic infections of CMV.

CMV infections in cells of the reproductive organs and in breast milk usually indicate infection in the mother by venereal pathways. It has been shown that a woman infected by the bacterium of gonorrhea is also likely to be infected with cytomegalovirus. There is a strong correlation of infection between these two agents of venereal disease.

Infection by cytomegalovirus in infants is a terrible disease for which there is no cure. Once herpesvirus invades body cells, the infection remains for life. It was said earlier that CMV infection in persons past puberty usually has symptoms that have temporary effects. In infants, CMV infection destroys body organs and tissues.

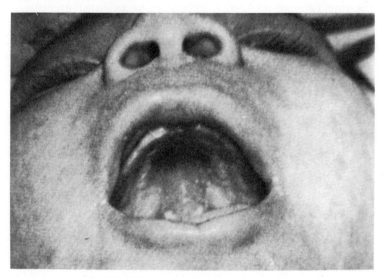

Fig. 6.1. *Herpes infection is serious in infants.*

Some of the devastating effects of this virus are not even treatable. The liver is the largest gland in the body and carries on biochemical activities that are necessary for life. The spleen is an organ that holds blood in reserve. Infection of CMV in infants often results in enlarged liver and spleen, reducing the usefulness of those organs. Another effect of this virus group is the rupturing of red blood cells, resulting in the yellowing of skin, a condition known as jaundice. Some infants are deformed, with abnormally small heads and brains, a condition called microcephaly. Peculiar spots on the skin due to capillary bleeding and an abnormal decrease in the number of blood platelets is another effect. (Capillaries are the smallest blood vessels in the body, which carry blood to all body tissues. Platelets are blood particles that are involved in the clotting process.)

Babies can be blinded permanently by the damage CMV viruses cause to the epithelial cells that cover the retina of the eye. A large number of infants suffer permanent brain damage from a buildup of calcium deposits in the cells of the cerebrum, which is the largest part of the brain. Many children infected with CMV as infants are blind, deaf, and mentally retarded. Venereal infection of the pregnant mother by cytomegalovirus has serious effects on the health of the newborn. Research teams are presently at work trying to find ways in which CMV infection can be cured.

Fig. 6.2. *A technician prepares a culture medium under a laminar flow hood (courtesy Burroughs Wellcome Company).*

Summary

Cytomegalovirus is a member of the herpesvirus group. The virus may enter the body through nonvenereal or venereal pathways. When a pregnant woman is infected with CMV, in all probability the fetus or the newborn will be infected with the virus. The effect of CMV infection in newborn babies may be deformity for life. Infection in adults causes temporary illnesses that return again and again.

Some Questions to Think About

1. Explain the meaning of "venereal pathway."
2. How does cytomegalovirus get into the body?
3. How does cytomegalovirus reproduce?
4. Why should pregnant mothers be tested for gonorrhea?
5. Why should free- health care be given to poor pregnant mothers?
6. Why does CMV have such terrible effects in infants?

CHAPTER VII

AIDS: The Insidious Epidemic

An epidemic is an uncontrolled spread of a particular disease. Epidemiologists are physicians who specialize in studying the spread of epidemics. How do these scientists determine when a disease has reached epidemic proportions? A tool essential to the work of the public health scientist is the use of numbers. Reported cases of a disease are counted and recorded to show accurate patterns of occurrence. When numbers are recorded in tables to demonstrate relationships between nonmathematical items, they are called *statistics*.

The Federal Centers for Disease Control in Atlanta, Georgia, and the National Institutes of Health in Bethesda, Maryland, have prepared statistics for a disease that has the shortened name of AIDS.

AIDS CASES REPORTED

Year	Number of Cases
1978	2
1979	7
1980	35
1981	185
1982	350
1983	2,950
1984	4,370
1985	9,150
1986	19,500
1987	40,000

AIDS: Acquired Immune Deficiency Syndrome

The table presents a statistical picture of the disease AIDS, which stands for acquired immune deficiency syndrome. You can see that over a nine-year period the number of reported cases has increased alarmingly. Notice that each year since 1978 the number has doubled.

Fig. 7.1 illustrates these statistics vividly, showing an increase of epidemic proportions in the number of reported cases.

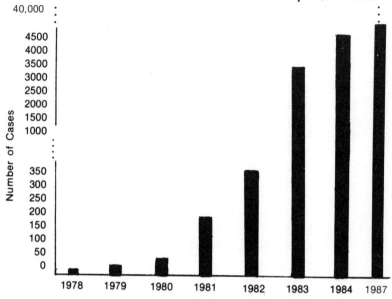

Fig. 7.1   *The number of AIDS cases reported 1978-1987.*

The table and the bar chart tell us how many cases of AIDS have occurred in the United States, but they do not tell us where the disease is most prevalent. The statistics that follow fill in another piece of the puzzle.

AIDS CASES REPORTED
January 1978 - August 1987

New York	20,500
California	19,400
Florida	500
New Jersey	175
Texas	100
Connecticut	75

The tables and the chart have supplied us with information concerning numbers and places. We now need to know who in the populations of New York, California, and other places are falling victim to acquired immune deficiency syndrome. The segment of a total population that is most prone to a disease is called the *target* population. The combined reports of epidemiologists, public health physicians, and local medical doctors indicate that the AIDS target population is made up of homosexual and bisexual males, intravenous drug abusers, hemophiliacs and others who have received blood transfusions, and babies born to women who are infected with AIDS.

AIDS: A Collection of Symptoms

As the name implies, acquired immune deficiency syndrome is a condition that involves the human immune system. Something happens that shuts down this system, leaving the body open to devastating infections. A syndrome is a collection of symptoms that accompany a particular condition. Scientists now know that AIDS is caused by a virus, the human immunodeficiency virus (HIV) that infects certain white blood cells and causes the immune system to collapse. It is also known that this virus enters the body through venereal pathways. Infected semen of one person delivers the virus into the body of another. Once in the anal or vaginal regions of the body, the virus makes contact with the bloodstream, where it becomes concentrated. The virus can also enter the bloodstream directly by transfusion with contaminated blood or by injection with HIV-infected needles.

SYMPTOMS OF AIDS

Overwhelming fatigue	Recurrent fever
Swollen lymph glands	Night sweats
Rapid weight loss	Purple skin tumors
Persistent cough	Lesions on skin
Coated tongue and throat	Easy bruising
Unexplained bleeding	Opportunistic diseases

The Immune System

The human body has an immune system that protects its cells, tissues, and organs against destruction by invading microorganisms. You know that the microorganisms that cause disease are commonly called germs. When germs enter the human body, cells of the immune system are called into action. Special white blood cells, lymphocytes, are produced in the bone marrow. They travel from the bone marrow into the bloodstream, where they remain quietly until stimulated by the presence of foreign particles (germs). Lymphocytes produced in the bone marrow are known as B cells. Another group of lymphocytes, produced in the thymus gland, are the T cells. The B lymphocytes and the T lymphocytes work together to destroy germs that invade body tissues.

Lymphocytes wage a two-pronged attack against disease-causing microorganisms. When germs get into the blood, the B cells enlarge in size and then divide. After division, the newly formed B cells secrete proteins known as *antibodies*, which act to prevent movement of the germ particles. The T cells differentiate (change) into two kinds of cells. Some of the T cells are helper cells, which not only help the B cells to produce antibodies, but also engulf the stilled germ cells. The other T cells, the suppressor cells, work against the helper cells, slowing down their activity.

The human body uses the technique of checks and balances in all of its biochemical activities. One set of chemicals, for example, speeds up a process; another set slows it down. Such checks and balances maintain *homeostasis*, or steady state control of body processes. Therefore the T helper lymphocytes encourage the work of the B cells, while the T suppressor cells discourage the activity of the T helper cells. This kind of control prevents the T helper cells from becoming so active that they destroy the blood proteins that are needed for normal functioning of the body.

Acquired immune deficiency syndrome does something to the immune system to prevent its normal functioning. Laboratory studies of the lymph (fluid without red blood cells) of AIDS patients reveal lymphocyte imbalance. Abnormal lymph has a larger number of T suppressor cells than T helper cells. (In normal lymph, the opposite is true; there are two and a half times more helper cells than suppressor cells.) As the suppressor cells outnumber the helper cells, the B lymphocytes cannot do their work and therefore become inactive. When the B cells are not working and the T helper cells become inactive, the entire immune system breaks down. Whenever the immune system does not work, the body is left unprotected against invasion by a host of disease organisms.

AIDS and Opportunistic Diseases

Tad was twenty-two years old, robust and seemingly in good health. Suddenly, with the ferocity of an exploding time bomb, he was struck down with an illness accompanied by many odd and frightening symptoms.

The first signs of his disorder were purple lumps, one appearing on each forearm. In rapid succession, these were followed by others until more than 60 unsightly but painless knots covered his upper body, neck, arms, and scalp. Other symptoms followed. Tad experienced severe diarrhea followed by extreme weight loss totaling nearly half his body weight. Elevated body temperature, swollen glands, and mouth sores contributed further stress to his weakened condition.

During hospitalization, Tad was treated with strong doses of antibiotics and antifungal drugs, which decreased the symptoms of illness. He became stronger and appeared well enough to be discharged from the hospital.

Two weeks after discharge, he became sick again, this time with a different set of symptoms. He labored under a painful shortness of breath brought about by water-filled lungs, and was exhausted by an extremely high fever. All of the hospital's resources and medications could not relieve these symptoms. Ten days after readmission, Tad died.

Tad's case study illustrates a pattern of illness that is becoming epidemic among young male homosexuals. The progression of illness follows a particular route. First of all, the immune system undergoes changes whereby the number of T helper cells decreases, upsetting the balance between helper lymphocytes and T suppressor cells. Initially, this imbalance between helper and suppressor cells can be detected only by clinical study of the lymph fluid.

As the decline in T helper cells continues, the immune system shuts down, becoming useless in its job of protection against invading organisms. What happens next is most unusual: The person becomes infected by organisms that usually do not harm the human body. Organisms such as these are called *opportunistic*, because they harm the human body only when the immune system fails to work. Why this is so puzzles epidemiologists. A brief description of some of the opportunistic organisms follows.

Candida albicans is a yeastlike fungus that causes thrush, an outbreak of small sores in and around the mouth. Candida usually infects children and has no ill effects on adults. However, when the immune system breaks down, *Candida albicans* causes serious infections in adults. The mildest of these are skin eruptions that occur in moist folds of skin on the arms, between the buttocks, around the nails, and in the armpits. More serious is the condition in which Candida invades the respiratory system, causing a lung infection that resembles tuberculosis. Candida may also damage the lining of the heart and destroy the linings that protect the brain. The systemic infection of Candida is difficult to treat, but sometimes it responds to nystatin, an antifungal antibiotic.

Toxoplasmosis is an infection of cells in the central nervous system, the spleen, the liver, and other organs. The germ responsible for this infection, *Toxoplasma gondii*, is something of a biological puzzle. It seems to be related to the animallike sporozoans (parasitic protozoa) and yet has some features resembling the plantlike fungi. It is a one-celled organism that invades the body and moves by gliding motions inside cells. Cysts and ulcerated sores come about when many toxoplasmas invade a single cell. The intact immune system prevents *T. gondii* from establishing itself in the body, because human lymphocytes are able to manufacture antibodies against it. When the immune system breaks down, the organism becomes a serious agent of infection.

Candida and Toxoplasma are not the only opportunistic germs. A kind of herpesvirus causes skin ulcers as large as a man's hand. A tuberculosislike bacterium usually found only in bats infects AIDS persons. Cryptosporidiosis, a parasitic infection of deer and other wild mammals, causes a death-dealing blow to immune-deficient humans. Other opportunistic infectious organisms are viruses of hepatitis A and B, atypical mycobacterium, the virus of meningitis, and various types of toxic (poisonous) bacteria.

The collapse of the immune system is the direct cause of illness. A person gets sick when his or her body cannot fight disease-producing organisms that infect the cells and tissues. Certain of these diseases signal the fact that the immune system has broken down. Such signal diseases are known as *markers*. The case study of Tad described two prevalent marker diseases, Kaposi's sarcoma and *Pneumocystis carinii* pneumonia (PCP).

Kaposi's Sarcoma

In 1872, Mortiz Kaposi, a Rumanian physician, first described the symptoms of the disease that now bears his name. In general, Kaposi's sarcoma is a condition in which cancerous tumors appear on many body sites at the same time. Doctors describe the condition as being "multifocal." Purplish nodules (little nodes or bumps) may erupt on the legs, arms, upper body, scalp, behind the ears, on the mucous membranes, and in many body organs. Kaposi's sarcoma shows itself in three different ways.

In Kenya, Tanzania, and Zaire, Kaposi's sarcoma (KS) is endemic. This means that it appears within populations in a certain geographical area but does not spread outward. In these three countries of equatorial Africa, KS is found among the native black population. Accounting for 9 percent of all malignant tumors, it is distributed through an age group of boys and young adult males under the age of 25 years. It is a rapid and an active disease, usually killing its victims in a short time. Kaposi's sarcoma is *not* of venereal origin in Africa. The exact mode of infection is not known.

Kaposi's sarcoma is not common among blacks in the United States. More commonly it occurs in older men of European descent, affecting greater numbers of men of Jewish or Italian ancestry. KS has been a slow disease, rarely becoming a problem.

Suddenly Kaposi's sarcoma has mushroomed into an epidemic among young homosexual males, striking down persons between the ages of 15 and 35 years. It is an active, fast-moving disease that kills about 20 percent of its victims. The symptoms of KS are severe weight loss, relentless diarrhea, purple-colored cancerous nodules, high and stubborn fever, thrush, swollen glands, and ulcerous body lesions. In many patients the symptoms of KS are reduced by treatment with strong doses of antibiotics and antifungal medications; however, easing those symptoms seems to leave the body open to a worse infection, *Pneumocystis carinii* pneumonia.

Pneumocystis Carinii Pneumonia (PCP)

Pneumocystis carinii pneumonia is caused by the infectious protozoan *Pneumocytis carinii*. This organism belongs to the group of parasitic protozoans known as sporozoans. *P. carinii* does not attack the human body when the immune system is intact, but it becomes a virulent killer when the immune system is inactive. This is so because the B lymphocytes cannot produce counteracting antibodies.

PCP may precede Kaposi's sarcoma or follow it. The symptoms of PCP are unexplained weight loss, persistent high fever, severe diarrhea, rashes in the mouth, shortness of breath, and water-filled lungs. The combination of KP sarcoma and PCP means certain death.

AIDS and Target Populations: What the Evidence Tells Us

Because AIDS is such a serious public health problem, many teams of scientists have been formed in research centers throughout the country to unravel the secrets of the mysterious HIV virus. Dr. James Curran heads the task force on Kaposi's Sarcoma and Opportunistic Infections at the Centers for Disease Control in Atlanta.

Epidemiologists have identified the populations in which most cases of AIDS occur, the AIDS target groups. The largest target group is that of homosexual and bisexual men. Homosexual men are attracted sexually to other men. Bisexual men take both men and women as sex partners. The HIV virus is passed from an infected person to another person during anal intercourse. It is known that the AIDS virus is carried in blood and semen. Infected semen can pass the virus to another when tissues in the rectal area are torn and contact with blood is made.

Almost equal in number to the homosexual/bisexual target group are the intravenous drug abusers. Men and women who inject illegal drugs into their veins and who share needles are rapidly falling victim to AIDS. Because the HIV virus is concentrated in the blood, a needle used by an infected person becomes the means by which the virus is passed to another.

Another target population consists of persons who have received transfusions of infected blood. Prior to 1985, before the AIDS virus was identified, infected blood was the source of AIDS in the population of heterosexuals who did not mainline drugs. Hemophiliacs are males who have inherited bleeder's disease. Their capillaries break, and blood is lost into the body tissues. Hemophiliacs require frequent transfusions of blood in order to live. Although blood is now scanned for the AIDS virus, 400 hemophiliacs (about 1 percent of the total AIDS cases) have been infected with AIDS.

Epidemiologists look for clues to where a focus of infection might be found. Such a clue was provided by babies infected at birth with AIDS but whose mothers were nondrug-abusing. It was found that a number of heterosexual women are married to bisexual men. In most cases these women are unaware of their husbands' double sex lives; however, the men infected their wives with the HIV virus and the women unknowingly pass it on to their unborn babies. It is estimated that about 4 percent of AIDS victims are heterosexual women who are not prostitutes and who do not mainline drugs. The clue of the infected babies brought to light the fact that the AIDS virus can be transmitted to women from infected sex partners. There is no explanation for the fact that female AIDS patients die much more rapidly than males.

AIDS Update: What Research Tells Us

Dr. C. Everett Koop, Surgeon General of the United States, agrees with the statistics that indicate that 1.5 million Americans carry the AIDS virus. Not all those who carry the virus have become sick with the disease. But Dr. Koop warns that if drastic means are not taken to contain the virus, by 1991 some 270,000 Americans will have contracted AIDS.

Although scientists know much more about the AIDS virus than was known in 1985, not enough is known about how the virus works. Physicians cannot prevent its killing effects. It is now known that the human immunodeficiency virus (HIV) destroys the immune system by invading and destroying certain white blood cells.

HIV is a retrovirus. This means that its genetic information is coded in RNA (ribonucleic acid) instead of in a DNA blueprint. Like other retroviruses, HIV produces an enzyme called *reverse transcriptase*, which assists the virus. When HIV enters a white blood cell called a T-4 lymphocyte, the virus captures the DNA of the infected cell. Reverse transcriptase instructs the DNA of the captured cell to make HIV virus particles, which ultimately destroy the host cell. Under usual circumstances, the information of heredity is coded in DNA. The codes in DNA are transferred to RNA, which helps to make proteins useful to the cell. Retroviruses reverse the process. Genetic instructions coded in RNA are transferred to DNA. Thus the cell makes more retroviruses instead of proteins.

According to immunologist Dr. Jeffrey Laurence of the Cornell University Medical Center, HIV behaves in strange ways. It can hide quietly in cells for a long time. Then something activates the virus. In its active state, HIV makes multiple copies of itself, which then destroy the cell. It is believed that the complication of HIV is caused by the presence of eight genes. It is usual for animal retroviruses to have three genes, which have been identified and named: *pol, env,* and *gag.* Pol provides the genetic blueprint that determines the characteristic enzymes of the virus. Gag is the code for the internal structure of the virus. Env is the gene that provides the genetic information concerning the structure of the outer virus coat. The outer coat is the part of the virus particle that determines what kinds of cell the virus can attach to and then enter.

The AIDS virus has eight genes. The functions of four of its genes are not known. Researchers Dr. William A. Haseltine of Harvard Medical School and Dr. Flossie Wong-Staal of the National Cancer Institute have discovered the function of an

Fig. 7.2   *The Virus of AIDS*

HIV gene called *tat*. Although they do not know how it works, they have discovered that tat can increase by several thousand times the cell's rate of production of new HIV viruses.

We now know that HIV retroviruses attack white blood cells known as T-4 lymphocytes. On their cell membranes the T-4 lymphocytes carry a protein known as OK T-4, or CD-4, or simply T-4. The T-4 protein acts as a receptor site for the AIDS virus, a specific spot on the cell membrane where the virus can enter the cell. Of recent discovery is the fact that the HIV virus can attack other cells also. The glial cells in the brain's gray matter are invaded by the virus, bringing on dementia (loss of mental ability), which has become a common symptom of AIDS. Part of the body's immune system involves white blood cells called monocytes and macrophages, which are scavenger cells that ingest foreign bacteria and virus particles. The HIV virus can infect these cells, destroying their ability to function as a defense against disease. Also destroyed by the AIDS virus are the endothelial cells that line and cover body organs.

Cells infected with the AIDS virus may change in a very unusual way. When the RNA of the retrovirus does not immediately stimulate the production of new virus particles, the infected cells stick together, forming large clumps of cells called *syncytia*. When these syncytia form, viral infection can be spread rapidly. The spreading of the virus to uninfected T-4 cells through the syncytia accounts for the rapid increase of HIV in infected persons.

Protection Against AIDS: The Surgeon General Speaks

Through a newspaper advertisement, the Metropolitan Life Insurance Company delivered this message: "AIDS IS SPREAD THROUGH BLOOD, SEMEN AND IGNORANCE." In this chapter, you have learned about the spread of AIDS through blood and semen. Now let us turn our attention to *ignorance*. Ignorance means not knowing. It was through the ignorance of her neighbors that the home of Louise Ray was burned to the ground. Mrs. Ray is the mother of three hemophiliac boys (age 8, 9, and 10) who acquired the AIDS virus through receiving transfusions of contaminated blood. Those folks in Arcadia, Florida, who burned out the Rays were ignorant of the mode of transmission of AIDS. They substituted violence for knowledge.

You know that AIDS is spread through venereal pathways and also by contact with infected blood. However, HIV is hard to catch. AIDS is not spread by casual contact. You cannot get AIDS from touching an infected person or even living in a close family setting. The AIDS virus is not carried in the air, nor is it transmitted by mosquito bite. AIDS is not spread by droplet infection as is the common cold, measles, or the flu.

Because people associate AIDS with blood, many have refused to donate blood to blood banks. AIDS is NOT passed on to blood donors. Blood is withdrawn from the veins in the arm by sterile needles. A sterile needle is one that is absolutely free of contamination. Once a needle is used, it is thrown away.

You Can Protect Yourself Against AIDS

Dr. Koop has recommended that people protect themselves against AIDS by following a few simple rules. Intravenous drug abusers should seek immediate help for their addiction. They should refrain from injecting themselves with illegal drugs and should not share needles. All people should avoid sex until marriage, and then they should have sex with only one partner. Dr. Koop is an advocate of "safe sex," which includes the use of condoms, rubber devices that prevent the virus of AIDS from being transmitted during sexual intercourse. Dr. Koop stresses education as the best weapon against the spread of the disease. He is also a compassionate man who believes in the civil rights of AIDS victims.

Summary

Acquired immune deficiency syndrome has become epidemic among homosexual/bisexual males and intravenous drug abusers. Four percent of the AIDS cases are heterosexuals. It is estimated that by 1991, 10 percent of all AIDS cases will be heterosexuals. HIV, the virus of AIDS, attacks cells in the immune system, causing its collapse. When the immune system stops functioning, the body can become infected by organisms that normally do not cause disease in humans. These diseases are described as opportunistic and they are killers.

The AIDS virus also attacks cells in the gray matter of the brain and infects tissue cells that line body organs. Currently, there is no vaccine that can prevent AIDS. A medication called AZT, azidothymidine, known under the trade name Retrovir, decreases some of the symptoms of AIDS. AZT has some side effects and is not a cure. Dr. Jonas Salk, who developed the vaccine that prevents polio, is now working on an AIDS vaccine. To date, the best protection against AIDS is knowledge.

Some Questions to Think About

1. Why is AIDS considered to be a collection of diseases and not a single disease?

2. With so many scientists working on the problem, why did it take so long to identify the virus that causes AIDS?
3. Why is *Pneumocystis carinii* pneumonia called an opportunistic disease?
4. What is the relationship between an opportunistic disease and a marker disease?
5. Why is it so difficult to develop a vaccine that will prevent AIDS?

CHAPTER VIII

Venereal Diseases of Varying Effect

AIDS, gonorrhea, syphilis, and genital herpes are considered to be major venereal diseases because they are widespread throughout human populations. Not only do these diseases infect great numbers of people, but also they are destructive of tissues and organs. There are other venereal diseases which, like gonorrhea, syphilis, and herpes, are transmitted through sexual contact. These diseases, however, are less common and less damaging to health.

Trichomoniasis

Trichomoniasis is a very common sexually transmitted disease. It is caused by a protozoan, *Trichomonas vaginalis,* which lives as a parasite in the vagina of females and in organs of the urinary tract in both sexes. The parasite causes inflammation of the vagina, resulting in a grayish, frothy, foul-smelling discharge and sometimes sores in the vagina. If the protozoans infect the fallopian tubes and the ovaries, the person feels pain in the lower abdominal region.

Although males are carriers of the disease, the infection usually causes the male very little distress. Complications are not known to arise from trichomoniasis; however, its effects are distressing to women. The best treatment known is a single oral dose of 2 grams of metronidazole, available under the trade name Flagyl.

Condylomata Acuminatum (Venereal Warts)

It is believed that a papilloma virus causes the growth of venereal warts, which resemble warts on other parts of the body. In the female, the warts develop around the hymen and

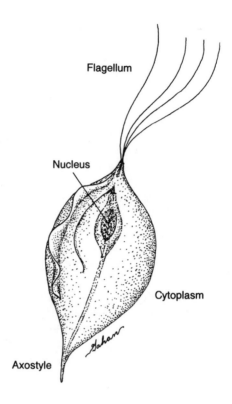

Fig. 8.1. Trichomonas vaginalis *is a protozoan that causes trichomoniasis.*

on the vulva. In the male, they appear on the head and shaft of the penis. Venereal warts are associated with poor genital hygiene. It is not uncommon for a person with these warts to have other venereal infections at the same time. Mild cases can be treated with an antiwart chemical. Severe cases require surgical removal. In some cases the warts become cancerous.

Pediculosis Pubis (Crab Lice)

The *Phthirus pubis,* a blood-sucking louse, is transmitted though pubic hair contact. This parasite is 1 to 4 cm long and cannot live more than 24 hours away from the human host. Infestation by these lice causes itching and rash in the pubic area. The treatment involves nothing more than cleanliness through the use of soap and water.

Scabies

Scabies can be transmitted by nonsexual and sexual contact. The female mite *Sarcoptes scabiei* burrows into the skin, depositing feces and eggs. In one to three months itchy, raised bumps develop. The itching often becomes unbearable. The condition is treated effectively by the use of the lotion benzyl benzoate applied to the skin.

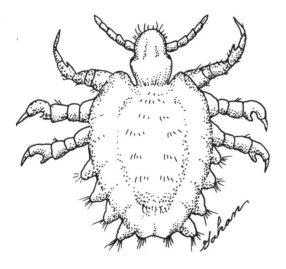

Fig. 8.2. Phthirus pubis *is the body louse that infests the pubic region.*

Monilial Vaginitis

Frequently the scientific names of diseases are puzzling to the layman; however, explanation of the meaning of a name helps to make the disease more understandable. *Monilia* is the

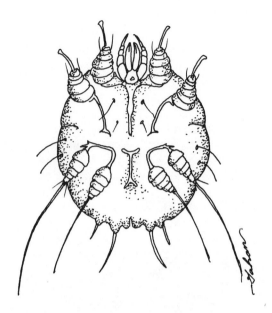

Fig. 8.3. Sarcoptes scabiei *is the mite that causes scabies.*

genus name of a group of fungi. A fungus is a non-green plant. Some fungi are infectious to humans. For example, ringworm and athlete's foot are caused by infectious fungi. These diseases are not classified as venereal because they do not affect the genital or urinary tract.

Monilial vaginitis is a fungus disease of the vagina. The causative fungus is the yeast *Candida albicans.* This fungus grows in the vagina and causes inflammation. Note that the suffix "itis" means inflammation of. *Candida albicans* grows very rapidly in the vagina, producing a thick discharge. As the organism spreads, it infects the vulva and causes pain and itching. At this stage the infection can be passed to a sex partner, who will probably develop an equally painful and itchy inflammation of the penis.

Several factors encourage the growth of *C. albicans.* Diseases include diabetes, chronic infectious diseases, and cancer.

Medications that increase the growth of the yeast are oral contraceptives, broad-spectrum antibiotics, and steroid drugs. Monilial vaginitis is a stubborn disease. Treatment involves use of antifungal drugs, careful cleansing of the skin, boiling of underwear, and frequent changes of clothing.

Nonspecific Urethritis (NSU)

Not too long ago a new group of infectious organisms called mycoplasmas were discovered. These microorganisms are similar to both bacteria and viruses. Some investigators believe that the mycoplasmas are responsible for the infection of the urethra known as nonspecific urethritis. As the name implies, there is no common agreement on the causative organism of this disease. However, the symptoms are unpleasant. The male usually has a strong discharge from the urethra and experiences pain when urinating. The female complains of urinary pain and burning and develops a thick vaginal discharge. The symptoms mimic gonorrhea, but the gonococcus is not present in cases of NSU. Tetracycline antibiotics are used in treatment.

SOME OTHER VENEREAL DISEASES

The diseases discussed in this section are found less commonly in the United States, appearing more frequently in tropical and subtropical climates. Modern means of transportation have reduced distances between continents and people, however, and infectious diseases tend to travel along with their carriers and are transmitted to others through sexual contact.

Chancroid

In 1859 the Italian dermatologist Augosto Ducrey discovered a bacillus that was given the scientific name *Hemophilus ducreyi*. This germ causes a venereal disease known as chancroid, or soft chancre. Chancroid is transmitted by sexual contact and for the most part found among prostitutes and the men who frequent them. Lack of bodily cleanliness seems to favor development of the infection.

The incubation period of the disease is very short. In three to five days after contact, an ulcerated sore develops on the genitals. This sore mimics the primary lesion of syphilis. The initial sore ruptures, leaving a circular ulcerated area. Many pustules then develop on the penis or on the vaginal lips. The person suffers persistent pain and inflammation of the genital organs. The lymph nodes drain pus.

Untreated chancroid develops into a serious condition. The repeated erupting of ulcerated sores and the failure of existing sores to heal causes the breakdown of genital tissue. Chronic chancroid infection can destroy part or all of the penis. The disease is best treated with sulfonamides. About 1,000 cases of chancroid are reported in the United States each year.

Lymphogranuloma Venereum

Lymphogranuloma venereum is a venereal disease that is quite common in tropical countries and increasing at an alarming rate in the United States. It is caused by an infectious parasite classified as a rickettsia, *Chlamydia trachomatis*, which resembles bacteria and viruses. Like bacteria, it has a rigid cell wall and can be destroyed by antibiotics. Like viruses, however, Chlamydia must reproduce inside cells.

Lymphogranuloma venereum is contracted through sexual intercourse with an infected partner. After multiplying within a cell, new Chlamydia particles are released and invade other cells. Infection is limited to epithelial cells of the genital tract and in the eyes and mouth. In women, mucous membranes in the vagina, cervix, and fallopian tubes are most vulnerable. In men, the infection occurs in the urethra, prostate gland, epididymis, and rectum. For persons whose immune system is functioning poorly, *C. trachomatis* causes a serious type of pneumonia. Chlamydia infection has a high incidence among the male homosexual population. It is interesting to note that the genus *Chlamydia* also contains the species of infectious organism that causes parrot fever and trachoma, an infectious blindness common in warm countries.

The incubation period is from five days to six weeks. A small sore appears on the penis or in the vagina and disappears after a short time. Next, the lymph glands in the groin swell and become painful. The infected lymph nodes fill with pus and drain through the skin.

The course of the disease varies. In some people it has little or no effect; in others, serious developments occur. The damage to the lymphatic system causes swelling and an accumulation of fluid known as edema. In some cases the disease continues for years and weakens the person to the state of invalidism. Gross enlargement of the infected genital organs causes a condition known as elephantiasis.

Lymphogranuloma venereum is diagnosed clinically by use of the Frei test. Antigens grown in egg yolk are placed under the skin. If swelling takes place in the area, it is a positive indication of infection. There is no specific treatment for the disease. The sulfonamides are helpful in the acute stages to alleviate the symptoms. Surgery is often used to remove enlarged body parts.

Granuloma Inguinale

Granuloma inguinale is by far the least prevalent of the venereal diseases. About 150 cases are reported each year. It occurs among the lower socioeconomic groups in the southern part of the United States. It is not especially contagious and is found, for the most part, in promiscuous persons who may have other venereal diseases.

The disease was first described by a Dr. Donovan in 1905 in India. He reported seeing rodlike inclusion bodies in tissue specimens taken from infected patients. The name given to this microorganism is *Donovania granulomatis*. The first sign of infection is a small pimple on the genital, thigh, or lower abdomen. Usually it spreads to other body parts by contact. The sores ulcerate and rarely heal; they become foul-smelling and very painful. If not treated, the disease may result in considerable destruction of the penis. It sometimes leads to death.

In the clinical laboratory, diagnosis is made by finding the characteristic "Donovan bodies" in tissue specimens taken from patients. The disease is most often treated with the tetracycline group of antibiotics. The sulfa drugs and penicillin are not effective for treatment of granuloma inguinale.

So few cases are reported each year without an increase in incidence that it is believed there is immunity to the disease. Because the organisms are difficult to culture outside of living tissue, not much is known about them.

Summary

The venereal diseases discussed in this chapter usually remain confined to the reproductive or urinary systems. Therefore they are best described as diseases of local infection. For the most part, the minor venereal diseases can be prevented by personal cleanliness and care in the selection of sex partners.

However, as was pointed out in Chapter VII, a contagious disease may become epidemic at any time. People whose lifestyles involve many different sexual partners are inviting multiple venereal disease infections. Promiscuous persons place themselves in the roles of disease transmitters. It is well to remember that a minor venereal disease of today has the potential to become tomorrow's major health problem.

Some Questions to Think About

1. What is meant by personal cleanliness?
2. Are all sores on the genitals due to venereal diseases? Give reasons for your answer.
3. What harm is there in contracting a minor venereal disease?
4. What kinds of organisms become parasites?
5. How may modern travel help to spread venereal diseases?
6. Why are some venereal diseases found more commonly in the tropics?
7. How can chancroid be confused with syphilis?

CHAPTER IX

Venereal Diseases of
Nonreproductive Organs

Sexually transmitted diseases are among the most common infectious diseases occurring in the United States today. Many of the infectious diseases that are passed from one person to another during sexual contact are bypassing organs of the urinary and reproductive tracts but infecting other organs. Such is the case of a form of viral hepatitis.

Hepatitis

Hepatitis is a viral infection of the liver. The infectious virus causes inflammation of liver tissue and some destruction of liver cells. The typical hepatitis starts with fever and shaking chills. Other symptoms follow, including loss of appetite, headache, and muscle pain. The upper abdomen is usually painful and tender and may exhibit muscle spasms. Sometimes joint pains and skin rashes occur. The liver becomes enlarged and tender. The urine becomes discolored with bile pigments. The skin takes on the yellow cast of jaundice. The afflicted person experiences periods of nausea, vomiting, and extreme fatigue. It is not unusual for the person to become irritable, despondent, and to lose the desire to do anything at all. These acute symptoms of hepatitis last from a few days to a few weeks. Complete recuperation takes several months.

This description of hepatitis is a general one. Actually, viral hepatitis refers to at least three separate diseases, each of which has a different cause, effect, and mode of prevention. However, the symptoms of these diseases are quite similar, and it was a long time before doctors learned to tell them apart. Now that they are recognized as separate diseases, their names have been changed accordingly. Hepatitis A was previously known as infectious hepatitis. Hepatitis B was known as serum hepatitis. A third type, called non-A, non-B viral hepatitis, has only recently been recognized. It is now known that hepatitis A and B may be sexually transmitted. Very recent clinical evidence shows that non-A, non-B viral hepatitis is also transmitted by sexual contact.

Hepatitis A

A person becomes infected with hepatitis A by ingesting a very small intestinal virus with food or water. Conditions of poor sanitation and close personal contact help spread this virus. Usually the virus travels from the feces of an infected person to the mouth of another person. This can happen through ingestion of contaminated food or water. Classic examples are the eating of contaminated clams or oysters. It can pass from one person to another through venereal pathways.

The incubation period for the disease is between 15 and 45 days. The disease usually begins abruptly with fever, listlessness, loss of appetite, nausea, abdominal pain, and jaundice. Very few people die from hepatitis A. In fact, the mortality rate is less than 1 percent.

Persons infected with hepatitis A excrete the virus in the stool. After jaundice appears, the chances of infecting others decrease. Antibodies develop in the blood as a result of this disease, and the person seems to have lifelong immunity after one attack.

Recent evidence indicates that hepatitis A may be sexually transmitted from one male homosexual to another via the anal-oral mode of sexual contact. The frequency of type A antibodies is greater in the male homosexual population.

The disease is not spread by droplet infection. Extremely low levels of the infectious virus have been found in urine. The spread of this disease is related to poor environment and poor personal hygiene.

Hepatitis B

Hepatitis B is caused by a larger, double-shelled virus known as the Dane particle. Infectious virus particles are often distinguished by protein markers called antigens. Hepatitis B has three such antigens or markers. One of the antigens is on the surface of the virus, another is in its core, and the third builds up in the blood serum of the infected person.

Hepatitis B has a very long incubation period—from four weeks to six months after the virus enters the body. The incubation period may be influenced by the amount of virus entering the body and the place of infection. The general health of the person also affects the incubation period. The symptoms of hepatitis B are similar to those of hepatitis A. However, the type B infection can result in polyarthritis and skin rashes. These conditions are caused by the surface antigen of the virus. Persons affected with hepatitis B often become carriers of the virus. It is estimated that there are 1 million such carriers in the United States. Carriers can remain infectious for years; a carrier may not show any signs of the disease but still can infect other people.

Hepatitis B can be spread from an infected person in many ways. The virus is in saliva, semen, urine, bile, blood serum, menstrual blood, vaginal secretions, abdominal fluid, and lung fluid. It is rarely found in feces. It is well known that hepatitis B is spread by use of infected hypodermic needles. Sexual activity is also a major factor in the transmission of this disease. The incidence of hepatitis B in the general population is greatest in the 15- to 29-year-old age group. This reflects both sexual transmission and drug abuse. Studies have shown that prostitutes have an exceptionally high prevalence of the hepatitis B surface antigen in their blood. This same antigen factor is found in 33 percent of the men who use the services of prostitutes, whereas in those who do not have sexual contact with prostitutes the antigen factor is less than 2 percent.

Hepatitis B antigens are found in patients attending VD clinics at the rate of 10 to 1 in the normal population. The risk of infection with hepatitis B increases with the number of sexual partners. Nearly half of homosexual men with more than 40 partners have evidence in their blood of current or prior infection with hepatitis B. Most of the patients with hepatitis markers in their blood have had gonorrhea or syphilis. The highest rates of hepatitis B blood markers occur in sexually active homosexual men, ranging upward to 51 percent. In this population, hepatitis B markers are related to multiple sex partners, prolonged periods of homosexual behavior, and a history of another sexually transmitted disease. The sexual transmission of hepatitis B probably occurs through the introduction of infectious viruses through epithelial surfaces of the body. Anal intercourse and oral sex are such methods of transmission.

Non-A, Non-B Hepatitis

One or more viruses may be the cause of non-A, non-B hepatitis. Hepatitis B and non-A, non-B have many symptoms in common. Both may cause chronic hepatitis and may give rise to the carrier condition.

Clinical evidence shows that non-A, non-B hepatitis may be transmitted sexually. The disease is seen in sexually active young adults. Interestingly, this disease is diagnosed by not finding markers for hepatitis A or hepatitis B. In other words, if clinical symptoms indicate that hepatitis infection has occurred, and if the antigen markers do not show the presence of type A or type B virus, it is assumed that the infection is non-A, non-B hepatitis.

Viral hepatitis is suspected in sexually active persons with symptoms of fever, listlessness, weakness, loss of appetite, nausea, vomiting, and jaundice. There is usually tenderness or pain in the upper abdomen. Patients with other diseases may have symptoms that imitate viral hepatitis. Syphilis is one such disease that may mimic viral hepatitis. Following exposure to any of these types of hepatitis, specific immune sera may be given. These may help to prevent the diseases or may lessen their effects.

SEXUALLY TRANSMITTED
INTESTINAL DISEASES

A major new public-health problem in some of the large cities of the United States has been recognized recently. There has been a sharp increase in three intestinal infections: amebiasis (a-mee-*bye*-a-sis), giardiasis (gee-ar-*dye*-a-sis) and shigellosis (shi-gel-*o*-sis). All three diseases are transmitted by sexual contact and are becoming quite common among the male homosexual populations of large cities. Amebiasis and giardiasis are caused by infectious protozoans. Shigellosis is caused by a pathogenic bacterium.

The intestinal diseases are usually acquired by taking in by mouth infectious material that has been contaminated by human feces. Contamination of this type is commonly associated with defective water and sewer systems or with poor conditions of hygiene. Traditionally, rural areas where primitive methods are used to dispose of human wastes have been the sources of serious intestinal diseases. *Shigella* bacteria are carried by flies from human feces or cow dung to milk and other foods. Drinking water contaminated by sewage has been the source of disease-producing protozoans that cause amebiasis or giardiasis. To a large extent, the rural areas of the United States now have modern and safer methods of waste disposal. The septic tank has replaced the outdoor privy, and wells that supply drinking water are protected against ground water seepage. With cleaner food and drinking water, it should be assumed that the spread of infectious intestinal diseases would be lessened.

It is now known that the microorganisms that cause intestinal disorders can live for long periods of time outside of the human body. These protozoans and bacteria lengthen their lives by an interesting device. They are able to form spores, that is, to wrap themselves in a thick cell wall that protects them against drying up in the outside environment. Oral sex practices of male homosexuals provide the means for spreading these organisms.

In New York City several case reports since 1982 have

focused attention on the fact that cases of intestinal illnesses caused by infectious protozoans and bacteria have been increasing. The increase of these diseases has been found to be within the sexually active homosexual community. In a sampling of 260 homosexuals who were treated at a particular clinic, there were 17 cases of amebiasis and 6 cases of shigellosis. In another clinic, of 38 men treated for shigellosis, 17 (45 percent) were homosexual. The homosexual population served by this hospital was quite small; therefore the percentage indicates the extent of the disease spread in a particular homosexual community.

Cases of shigellosis and amebiasis have also increased in the homosexual community in San Francisco. In a study, contaminated food was ruled out as the source of infection, and it was established that among these males there was frequent oral-anal and oral-genital contact. To date, the most searching study of the incidence of intestinal protozoan infections among homosexual males was undertaken recently at a clinic that treated only homosexually active males. This clinic served as a screening facility for syphilis and gonorrhea. Participating in the study were the Bureau of Venereal Disease Control and the Division of Tropical Diseases of the New York City Health Department. Examination of the stools of 89 males showed that 26 percent contained protozoan pathogens. All of these men practiced anal-lingus. The 74 percent of the group who did not have these pathogens did not practice anal-lingus. Travel outside the United States was ruled out as a factor in the results.

Amebiasis

Amebiasis is caused by the protozoan *Entamoeba histolytica*. It is commonly known as the dysentery ameba and was first identified by Losch in Russia in 1875. *E. histolytica* normally lives in the intestinal wall of humans, where it causes ulceration of tissue. Examination of the food vacuoles in this protozoan reveals that they contain red blood cells, white blood cells, and other tissue fragments. This is evidence of the extent to which *E. histolytica* parasitizes human tissues. It also lodges in the lung, brain, and testis. When these organs are infected, the disease is known as amebiasis. Amebic dysentery refers to infection in the intestines.

The mature ameba is rather large and has a granular cytoplasm. Under certain conditions, *E. histolytica* undergoes a series of mitotic cell divisions, producing eight very small cells. Each cell encysts. In this form it passes out of the body of the host in the feces. When a cyst enters another human host, the heavy cell wall dissolves and the organism grows to full size. The mature ameba burrows in the wall of the intestine and parasitizes the new host.

Symptoms of amebiasis may be mild or severe. In most cases, the infected person experiences diarrhea, nausea, vomiting, loss of appetite, and elevated temperature. Since these are the symptoms of many diseases, the doctor has to have

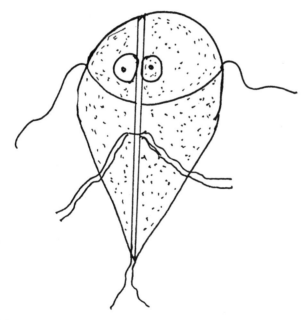

Fig. 9.1. Giardia enterica, *a front view. Note the four pairs of flagella and the central axostyle.*

stool specimens examined for the presence of the organism. When the general health of the person is poor, this disease can have serious consequences.

Giardiasis

Giardia enterica is a one-celled organism that is parasitic in human intestines. *G. enterica* has two nuclei, two axostyles, four pairs of flagella, and a sucking disk on its underside. This protozoan reproduces by binary fission and also forms spores that are able to live for a long time outside the human host.

Infection by *G. enterica* is known as giardiasis. The symptoms are similar to those caused by *E. histolytica*. A diagnostic laboratory examination is necessary to tell the difference between the two diseases.

Shigellosis

The genus *Shigella* contains a number of organisms that cause intestinal disorders in humans, some very mild, others severe. *S. dysenteriae* causes a serious illness in which there is extensive inflammation and ulceration of the large bowel. Other of the shigellas cause mild diarrhea. The shigellas are bacteria and, like the typhoid organisms, contaminate water and food.

Why the Concern?

Public health is of great concern. An infectious disease that is found in one part of the population does not remain isolated there. Disease-producing organisms tend to spread. If the number of cases of shigellosis, amebiasis, and giardiasis is increasing in the male homosexual population, these diseases will also appear in the general population. Of concern is not the sexual preferences of a part of the population, but the *pattern* by which diseases are spread. Heterosexuals who have oral-anal contact and who have many sex partners also will contract and transmit the intestinal diseases.

You may ask how an infection that passes by way of the oral-fecal route can reach those who are not promiscuous. You have only to think of the numbers of people who handle the food that you eat to realize that intestinal infection is not far removed from any one person. Although food handlers are supposed to be checked for enteric (intestinal) organisms, we know that many "off the books" workers are not included in health code regulations. Think of all of the foods you eat in a day or a week that are handled by someone else: the unwrapped rolls that you buy, the hot dog from the street vendor, the ice cream cone from the corner candy store, the restaurant meals. All are possible sources of infection. A member of your own family might be a source of infection. We cannot see microorganisms with the naked eye and therefore cannot determine their presence by casual inspection. Our best protection from infectious organisms is awareness.

Some Questions To Think About

1. Rarely does hepatitis kill a person. Why should we worry about this disease?
2. Why are organisms that form cysts dangerous?
3. Why should a person's travel patterns be considered when tracing the source of an enteric disease?

CHAPTER X

VD and the Adolescent

"RECOMMEND EARLY ED
IN BIRTH CONTROL

Half of all teenage pregnancies occur in the first six months of sexual activity, so the best way to prevent these pregnancies it to give birth control information to girls before they begin having intercourse . . . "

New York *Daily News*

The Teenager and Sex

The involvement of today's youth in sexual activities is a serious matter. A strong society is one in which the energy of youth is used to develop special knowledge and skills that are needed for the world of work. When young people become involved in sex too early in life, it seems to drain off the energy that ought to be used in developing intellectual ability. There is much to be said for the postponing of sexual activity until one has reached a level of maturity in which a true love relationship is formed.

As the news item fragment above indicates, the adult population is responsible for the premature sexual activity of youth. Young people are bombarded with the propaganda that supports the myth that early sex is natural and acceptable. For example, a recent movie labeled by critics as "refreshing" and "appealing" centered on a 43-year-old divorced man and his 17-year-old mistress. Maybe this film was dubbed "refreshing" because she was still attending high school! Urging sex upon young people in advertising, television shows, popular songs, newspaper articles, and the like demonstrates a kind of sickness in our society that sociologists seem reluctant to deal with. When young people are duped into believing that sexual activity among their peers is not harmful, they are being directed toward a life pattern that is degrading and unhealthful.

At some time someone has to be truthful enough to say that sexual activity is not for children and young teenagers. Promiscuity of youth is destructive of mind and body. Good health depends upon what a person does with his or her life. The venereal diseases are a group of infectious diseases that measure the quality of one's life. Every person infected with VD has contracted it by having sexual contact with an infected partner. Sixty-four percent of the reported cases of venereal disease occur among young people between the ages of 14 and 21. Sexual promiscuity is the major factor leading to venereal disease.

"Doing one's thing" is a popular philosophy that seems to direct the behavior of many people today. An increasing number of middle-aged people and many young persons are advocates of this life philosophy that rejects standards and structure. Doing what we feel like doing when we feel like doing it is usually not the best course of action. Loose, unstructured living is of questionable value to the individual and to society. Certain rules of behavior are necessary to establish positive relationships between the sexes. In fact, every culture and every society has found it necessary to devise rules of behavior that serve the best interests of all.

The society in which we live endorses a monogamous way of life. *Monogamy* means that each adult may have only one marriage partner at one time. This implies that an *adult* should have one sexual partner at one time. In most societies the most important rules of behavior are set down in written laws. Some aspects of behavior are governed by unwritten codes, because it is not possible to set down all of the facets of life in writing. Our society has both written and unwritten rules.

Many of the social problems confronting our communities are the result of the failure of people to obey the rules. The cultural turmoil of the 1960's paved the way for the trend in thinking that upholds personal disobedience and the breaking of many codes of behavior. The discarding of outmoded rules makes sense only when they are replaced by better ones. It is not a better way of life when people, young or older, engage in sexual activities with many partners. In 1987 an alarming number of babies were being born with AIDS.

A kind of sickness seems to be increasing in the adult society. Many young children are being exploited sexually, both within and outside of family groups. Following is an except from a newspaper article describing the kind of abuse to which some children are subjected.

"CHARGE CITY TEACHER
IN SALE OF KIDDIE PORN

An . . . elementary school teacher was charged with selling and distributing photographs showing young boys in various explicit sexual acts, the FBI announced. . . . FBI agents said they found a small truckload of pornographic material mostly involving children. Federal agents confiscated photos of boys aged 9 through 12 engaged in sexual acts . . . "

Children who are thus abused sexually do not have the right even to choose the direction of their lives. Most such children become social and psychological misfits in whom deviant sexual behavior is the focus of life.

The Meaning of Puberty

When boys and girls reach the age of 13 or 14, their sex glands begin to become active. The testes of males begin to produce sperm cells, and the ovaries of females produce mature eggs. Male sex glands produce male hormones, and the ovaries secrete female hormones. Both male and female hormones guide the development of secondary sex characteristics. The boy's voice becomes deeper, his arms become more muscular, he loses his "baby fat," and he begins to think about shaving and about girls. Girls go through bodily and mental changes also. Their breasts begin to develop and their hips round out. Menstruation begins and the girls, of course, think about boys. All of these body changes and thoughts of the opposite sex are normal.

Puberty means that a boy or girl is reaching sexual maturity; however, teenagers are not legally, socially, or emotionally mature. They are still dependent upon their parents for help and protection. Most adolescent boys and girls are not in a position to take on adult responsibilities such as having children and raising a family. The sex practices of teenagers usually lead to unwanted children, which must be supported by a Department of Welfare, and venereal disease, which may or may not be treated. The New York City Department of Health operates many free clinics that treat VD exclusively. It is estimated that less than 50 percent of those with VD are under treatment. You now know that syphilis and gonorrhea are serious diseases. If they are left untreated, they can kill. You also know that babies born with syphilis may be blind or brain-damaged or deformed in other ways. You know that AIDS kills.

Some "Old-Fashioned" But Sound Philosophy

The teenage years should be happy and productive years. This should be a time when the young person is preparing for adult life, going to high school to prepare for further schooling or for the world of work. During the adolescent years, teenagers are free from adult responsibilities, and they should use this time to explore their unique capabilities and talents. This is the only time in life when boys and girls have the opportunity and energy to think about and learn about fields of endeavor that might become their life's work. Adolescence is the time of life when one's potential should be developed.

Experimenting with sex complicates matters. Experimenting with sex is not the same as practicing the piano, or training in a sport, or learning Spanish, or learning to paint in oils, or doing any of the number of productive things that can make you a better person. When you become involved in sexual relationships too early, you are short-changing yourself. You are limiting your opportunities to find the person that you really are. To develop into a psychologically mature and contented adult takes time. Young college people are beginning to find out that "living together" really does not work out well in our society. One of the sex partners usually exploits and uses the other. There is no equality in such a relationship if one benefits at the expense of the other. A young person who does not think enough of himself or herself to do things properly invites personal disaster.

In her last year of high school, Bridget gave birth to a baby girl. The father of the child broke his promise to her and married someone else. Bridget's classmates either went on to college or went to work. Bridget went on welfare.

They called him "L.B." for Lover Boy. To be sure, he "made out" with an untold number of girls. He graphically described his exploits to the boys who hung out in front of the pizza parlor. L.B. did not share the knowledge that the rash on his body was a sign of syphilis nor that his dripping penis signaled gonorrhea.

People who are in a position to evaluate behavior (doctors, teachers, lawyers, religious leaders, parents) agree that promiscuity decreases the quality of one's life. Aside from contracting VD and running the risk of unwanted pregnancy, there is another serious danger. A promiscuous person may develop emotional problems that lead to instability. Unstable people do not remain married, nor do they contribute to others on an adult level. Sexual maturity develops when one follows the rules for growing up. A teenage life should be used to develop skills for future work, good health practices, moral responsibility, and the drive to work for personal achievement.

About Homosexuality

Thus far, in this chapter, we have considered sexual relations between persons of opposite sexes. In Chapter VII the health hazard faced by male homosexuals was discussed. Female homosexuals seem not to be plagued by AIDS. Our concern here is not only for good health practices, but also for the social-sexual-biological choices that you must make. Recently, much publicity has been generated about men and women who have sexual preferences for others of their own sex. In terms of the biology of species, homosexuality is not a useful practice for many-celled organisms. Perpetuation of all vertebrate species depends upon the fertilization of an egg cell by sperm. This can be accomplished only by male and female sex partners.

Socially and psychologically, however, homosexuality may better meet the needs of some persons. Why this may be so is not a question that can be answered in this book. However, it must be stated that high incidences of all venereal diseases occur in the homosexual population. In addition, other diseases that are transmitted sexually are increasing rapidly among homosexuals. The high rate of VD may be due to the fact that homosexuals change sex partners often. There is a tendency for homosexuals to have sexual contacts with others whom they don't even know. Promiscuous homosexuals spread VD from one sex contact to another just as promiscuous heterosexuals do. It is only fair to mention that not all homosexuals are promiscuous. Some form a steady relationship with one partner. In such stable relationships the incidence of venereal disease is low.

Some Questions to Think About

1. How can VD change the direction of a young person's life?
2. Why should teenagers avoid involvement in sex?
3. How should the topic of venereal disease be handled at home and at school?
4. Why is the rate of VD exceptionally high among male homosexuals?

CHAPTER XI

Question and Answer Wrap-up

Can you get syphilis from kissing?
The most common way to contract syphilis is through sexual intercourse. But if the person happens to have a chancre in the mouth, you can become infected.

Can a person get syphilis from a toilet seat?
No. And you can't get it from using someone's towel, or from a drinking glass.

How would I know if I had syphilis?
A woman may have a painless sore in or near the vagina; this may be a sign of syphilis. A male may have a hard, painless sore on the penis; it can sometimes appear on the lip, in the mouth, or around the rectum. The sore is called a chancre. While moist, the chancre is highly infectious. Without treatment, the chancre will heal in a few weeks. This is the first stage of syphilis.

What are the symptoms of syphilis in the second stage?
A common symptom is a rash all over the body; although it looks like measles, it doesn't itch. Other signs are lesions in the mouth or a rash on the hands and feet. Moist rash or sores are usually infectious.

Can you have syphilis and not know it?
Certainly. The symptoms don't appear for about three to six weeks, and then they disappear after a few weeks. Even after the secondary skin rash disappears, the infection remains and the problem becomes worse.

What can untreated syphilis do to a person?
In time, it can destroy the cells in your brain or destroy your spinal cord. It may damage your heart and blood vessels. Thus it can drive you insane, paralyze you, or cripple you.

Is it harder for a female to get syphilis than for a male?
No. But it's harder for a female to know that she has it. The sores are sometimes hidden in the walls of the vagina.

Can you die from syphilis?
The disease works slowly. It can take years. Some 15 to 25 percent of those who do not have syphilis treated die prematurely.

If a pregnant woman has syphilis, will her baby be born with the disease?
If she does not get treatment, she may never have the baby. Syphilis may cause a miscarriage. But if she does have the baby, the odds are that it will have the infection.

Is syphilis easy to cure?
Yes, especially in the early stages. A series of penicillin shots is all it takes; however, many people don't bother to get the shots or don't finish the series.

How does a person find out if he or she has syphilis?
You go to a doctor's office or a public health clinic for a test. If you go to a clinic, chances are there will be no charge.

Can teenagers go to a doctor for treatment without having their parents informed?
It depends on the law in your state. In some states, if you're a minor, a doctor is free to treat you without the consent of your parents. In other states, it is against the law for a doctor to treat you without your parents' consent. To find out the law in your state, call your local department of health. The number is in the phone book.

What is the test for syphilis?
If a sore is present, a smear is taken and examined under a microscope. Otherwise, a blood test is given. A sample of blood is taken from your arm as it would be for any other blood test. The sample is sent to a laboratory, and you will be able to get the results in a couple of days.

If a condom is used, can a person prevent contracting syphilis?
A condom provides some protection, because penis and vagina contact is avoided. But it is no sure guarantee against infection. There can still be contact during foreplay.

Is there anything else I can do to protect myself?
Yes. Wash your genital area with soap and water before and after intercourse (that goes for your partner, too). The soap and water washes away some of the germs. It helps to urinate after intercourse; the urine also washes away some of the germs. Again, these steps are no guarantee against the disease, but they will reduce the chance of infection.

Can only prostitutes get syphilis?
Anybody can get it, but the truth is that "nice kids" are more likely to get it. For a prostitute, syphilis can interfere with her career, so she is more likely to know what signs to look for and what to do about them. This doesn't mean that you can't contract syphilis from a prostitute. You can, and many people do. Prostitutes continue to be carriers of the disease, so contact with one is still taking a chance.

Is is possible to get syphilis from someone of your own sex?
If the person is infected and you have sexual contact, the answer is yes.

Can the disease be passed on only when the chancre is showing?
No. The disease may be transmitted after the chancre

disappears. It may also be transmitted in the secondary
stage when there are moist lesions.

Once you're cured, do you become immune to syphilis?
No. Having syphilis once is no guarantee you won't get
it again.

Do you get syphilis just by having a lot of sex?
If your partner doesn't have syphilis, you can't get the
disease, no matter how often you have sex. However, if you
have sex with a lot of different partners, your chances of
coming in contact with an infected person are greater.

Which disease is worse, syphilis or gonorrhea?
Syphilis is the more damaging of the two if not treated
promptly, but gonorrhea is also harmful.

Which disease is more common?
Gonorrhea is 20 times more common than syphilis. The
number of cases keeps increasing, particularly among
women, in whom the symptoms of the disease are harder to
spot.

How do you get gonorrhea?
The same way you get syphilis: through sexual contact with
someone who already has the disease.

Can you have gonorrhea and not know it?
If you're a female, you may not know it. Four out of five
women show no symptoms; one out of five may have a
vaginal discharge. However, one man out of five shows no
symptoms either. If you've been exposed and have no
symptoms, you should have a doctor examine you.

What are the signs in the male?
He usually has a painful, burning sensation when he uri-
nates and a smelly yellow-white discharge from his penis.

What are the signs in a female?

In most cases there are no outward signs—no pain, no discharge, nothing. Public health authorities say four women out of five who have gonorrhea show no immediate signs at all. Right now there are at least 2 million people walking around with gonorrhea, and most of them don't know it.

What can gonorrhea do to people?

Without treatment, it can ruin you in a lot of ways. It can make you sterile. If you're a male, it can damage your sperm ducts. If you're a female, it can damage your fallopian tubes. If you should have the germs on your hands and accidentally rub your eyes, you could find yourself with a serious eye infection. It can also lead to a crippling form of arthritis, meningitis, or heart disease.

How long does it take for gonorrhea to appear?

Three to five days.

How does a doctor test for gonorrhea?

In a male, he takes a smear of the discharge and examines it under a microscope. He usually can tell immediately. In doubtful cases he may send it to a lab for testing. In a female, the test is simple, too. The doctor swabs the vagina and sends the sample to a laboratory for testing. The results are returned in a couple of days. Because it is possible to have syphilis and gonorrhea at the same time, a doctor usually takes a blood sample to test for syphilis when testing for gonorrhea.

Will a doctor ever treat a female for gonorrhea even though the lab tests are negative?

Yes. The signs of gonorrhea in the female are difficult to spot. If a girl has had contact with a diagnosed case of gonorrhea, she often is treated regardless of the lab results. The discomfort of having one or two shots is better than having to suffer the agonies of gonorrhea later.

Can't you detect gonorrhea through a blood test?
No. There is, as yet, no blood test for gonorrhea.

Can you get gonorrhea from kissing?
Generally, no.

Can you get gonorrhea from not bathing?
No. It has nothing to do with lack of hygiene. All the gonorrhea germ needs is direct contact with the mucous area of the genital organs. However, washing the genital area with soap and water before and after intercourse will wash away and kill many of the gonorrhea germs. Urinating after intercourse will also wash away some of the germs.

If a condom is used, am I safe?
As in the case of syphilis, you're safer than if you don't use one, and for the same reason—you avoid penis and vagina contact. But there is no guarantee against the infection.

Can gonorrhea lead to syphilis? Or the other way around?
No, they are separate diseases.

If I have gonorrhea and it's cured, can I get it again?
Yes. You can get it again, many times. There is no immunity against gonorrhea. Having sex with someone who has the infection is all it takes.

Does a discharge from the penis (or vagina) always mean gonorrhea?
No, not always. But you'd better check it out with a doctor. It could still mean trouble.

Isn't it gonorrhea that can be contracted from a toilet seat, but not syphilis?
No. It takes sexual contact with a person who has the infection to contract the disease.

Are birth control pills any protection against gonorrhea?
No. They may prevent pregnancy, but not VD.

If I am homosexual, can I get gonorrhea?
Yes. The symptoms can appear in the rectal area as well as in the genital organs.

I thought you were tested for gonorrhea before being married?
No. You are tested for syphilis by a blood test. But as we said before, there is no blood test for gonorrhea.

If I have VD, what should I do about others who may be infected?
If you have been disagnosed and are undergoing treatment for VD, don't conceal the names of your sexual partners. You're not doing them a favor. The chances are that one of them infected you or that you have given them VD. Early diagnosis and treatment are important, so names and addresses should be given to medical and public health workers. It's their job to give confidential treatment for VD and help stop the spread of the disease.

How can I tell if my sex partner has herpes?
One telltale sign of genital herpes is the presence of blistery sores on and around the genital area. Sometimes a person can be contagious without having blistery sores. There is no foolproof way to tell when a silent carrier is shedding the virus.

Does genital herpes cause cancer?
There is evidence that women with genital herpes are more likely to develop cancer of the cervix than those who have not had the infection.

If there is no cure for herpes, why should I see a doctor?
You may have symptoms of another disease that mimics herpes and can be treated. Only a doctor is capable of

making this diagnosis. New therapy has recently become available to doctors for the management of initial genital herpes.

How does herpes affect babies?
A baby can become infected from its mother. Many infected babies die or suffer brain damage.

If I touch a person who has AIDS, will I get the disease?
No. Evidence indicates that AIDS is transmitted through sexual intercourse between male homosexuals involving sperm and blood.

If I donate blood, can I contract AIDS?
No. Blood donors cannot be infected by AIDS organisms. Persons tranfused with AIDS-infected blood can get the disease.

Can male homosexuals protect themselves against contracting AIDS?
Physicians suggest that they should use a condom during intercourse and should avoid the use of nitrate drugs.

Can a pregnant mother transmit *Chlamydia trachomatis* to her baby?
The infection is passed from mother to child during birth.

What effect does *Chlamydia trachomatis* infection have on babies?
The infection can cause blindness in babies. It can also cause a type of pneumonia that resists treatment by antibiotics and thus causes death.

Where can I get more information about AIDS?
You can call toll-free 1-800-342-AIDS, 24 hours a day, 7 days a week. You can write to AIDS, P.O. Box 14252, Washington, DC 20044, requesting a copy of the "Surgeon General's Report on Acquired Immune Deficiency Syndrome."

APPENDIX A

Where to Get Help

1. For a list of clinics at which VD help may be obtained all over the United States, write to:

   > Public Health Service
   > Communicable Disease Center
   > Venereal Disease Branch
   > Atlanta, Georgia 30333

2. For the Department of Public Health in your state, consult the telephone book.

   If you live in New York State, contact:

   > New York State Department of Health
   > Venereal Disease Control
   > (518) 474-3595

3. If you live in New York City, contact Planned Parenthood, 300 Park Avenue South, New York, N.Y. 10010. Telephone 677-3320

   New York City Health Department Clinics:

Manhattan

Central Harlem
2238 Fifth Avenue
(137th Street)
690-0606

Chelsea
303 Ninth Avenue
(28th Street)
239-1700

East Harlem
158 East 115th Street
(off Lexington Avenue)
876-0300

Riverside
160 West 100th Street
(Between Columbus and
Amsterdam)
866-8785

Bronx

Morrisania
1309 Fulton Avenue
(East 169th Street off
Third Avenue)
992-4200

Richmond

51 Stuyvesant Place
(Wall Street)
St. George, S.I.
727-6000

Brooklyn

Brownsville
259 Bristol Street
(Blake and Dumont
Avenues)
495-7240

Crown Heights
1218 Prospect Place
(Troy Avenue)
757-0507

Fort Greene
295 Flatbush Avenue
Extension
(Willoughby Avenue)
643-8351

Queens

Corona
34-33 Junction Boulevard
(Roosevelt and Northern)
476-7620

Jamaica
90-37 Parsons Boulevard
(off Jamaica Avenue)
658-6600

Rockaway
67-10 Rockaway Beach
Boulevard
474-2100

Health departments in major cities:

Atlanta, Georgia	(404) 656-4937
Augusta, Maine	(207) 289-1110
Austin, Texas	(512) 454-3781
Baltimore, Maryland	(301) 383-2644
Boston, Massachusetts	(617) 727-2681
Chicago, Illinois	(312) 793-2793
Columbus, Ohio	(614) 461-7367
Denver, Colorado	(303) 388-6111
Detroit, Michigan	(313) 872-1540
Frankfort, Kentucky	(502) 564-4935
Harrisburg, Pennsylvania	(717) 787-8842
Hartford, Connecticut	(203) 566-4140
Honolulu, Hawaii	(808) 548-2211
Indianapolis, Indiana	(317) 633-6310
Jackson, Mississippi	(904) 354-3961
Jefferson City, Missouri	(314) 635-4111
Juneau, Alaska	(907) 586-5301
Los Angeles, California	(213) 620-2900
Minneapolis, Minnesota	(612) 378-1150
Montgomery, Alabama	(205) 269-7606
Nashville, Tennessee	(615) 741-3614
New Orleans, Louisiana	(504) 527-5816
New York, New York	(212) 971-5647
Oklahoma City, Oklahoma	(405) 427-6561
Olympia, Washington	(206) 753-5900
Phoenix, Arizona	(602) 271-4521
Philadelphia, Pennsylvania	(215) 238-7703
Raleigh, North Carolina	(919) 829-3419
Richmond, Virginia	(703) 770-6265
San Diego, California	(714) 232-4361
San Francisco, California	(415) 843-7900
Santa Fe, New Mexico	(505) 827-2107
Trenton, New Jersey	(609) 292-4027
Washington, D.C.	(202) 655-4000

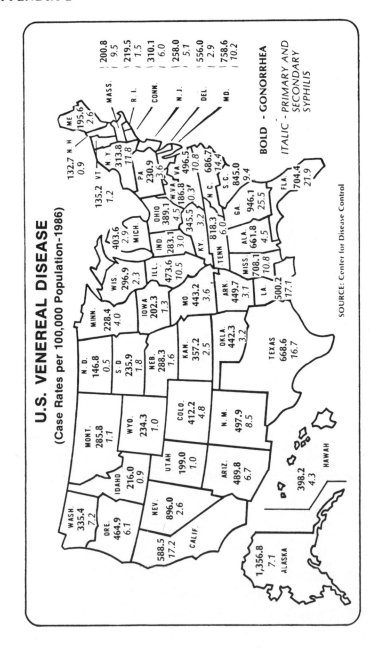

U.S. VENEREAL DISEASE
(Case Rates per 100,000 Population—1986)

BOLD - GONORRHEA

ITALIC - PRIMARY AND SECONDARY SYPHILIS

MASS.	**200.8**	*9.5*
R. I.	**219.5**	*1.5*
CONN.	**310.1**	*6.0*
N. J.	**258.0**	*5.1*
DEL.	**556.0**	*2.9*
MD.	**758.6**	*10.2*

ME. **195.6** *2.6*

N. H. **132.7** *0.9*

VT. **135.2** *1.2*

N.Y. **313.8** *11.8*

PA. **230.9** *3.6*

W.VA. **186.8** *0.3*

VA. **496.5** *10.8*

N.C. **686.7** *14.4*

S.C. **845.0** *9.4*

FLA. **704.4** *21.9*

GA. **946.1** *25.5*

ALA. **661.8** *4.5*

TENN. **818.3** *6.0*

MISS. **708.1** *10.8*

LA. **500.2** *17.1*

OHIO **389.1** *3.0*

KY. **345.5** *3.2*

IND. **283.1** *3.0*

ILL. **473.6** *10.5*

MICH. **403.6** *2.9*

WIS. **296.9** *2.3*

MINN. **228.4** *4.0*

IOWA **202.3** *1.3*

MO. **443.2** *3.6*

ARK. **449.7** *3.1*

N.D. **146.8** *0.5*

S.D. **235.9** *1.8*

NEB. **288.3** *1.6*

KAN. **357.2** *2.5*

OKLA. **442.3** *3.2*

TEXAS **668.6** *16.7*

MONT. **285.8** *1.1*

WYO. **234.3** *1.0*

COLO. **412.2** *4.8*

N.M. **497.9** *8.5*

IDAHO **216.0** *0.9*

UTAH **199.0** *1.0*

ARIZ. **489.8** *6.7*

WASH. **335.4** *7.2*

ORE. **464.9** *6.1*

NEV. **896.0** *2.6*

CALIF. **588.5** *17.2*

ALASKA **1,356.8** *7.1*

HAWAII **398.2** *4.3*

SOURCE: Center for Disease Control

108

STD in the Male Homosexual Community

Disease Name	Causative Organism	Sites of Infection	Symptoms
Syphilis	*Treponema pallidum* (spirochete)	penis, rectum, lips, anus	rectal discharge, bleeding, lesions, chancres on tongue, around mouth, rectum
Gonorrhea	*Neisseria gonorrhoeae* (bacterium)	anus, throat	anal discharge, bloody mucous, sore throat, tonsil inflammation
Amebiasis	*Entamoeba histolytica* (protozoan)	alimentary canal, small and large intestine	diarrhea, abdominal cramps, fever, chills, bloody stools
Giardiasis	*Giardia enterica* (protist)	intestines	diarrhea, weight loss, abdominal pain
Shigellosis	*Shigella dysenteriae* (bacterium)	intestines	nausea, vomiting, bloody stools, diarrhea, pain in the abdomen, dehydration
Salmonellosis	Salmonella strains	intestines	nausea, vomiting, abdominal pain, diarrhea
Hepatitis A	Hepatitis virus A	liver	fever, chills, loss of appetite, headache, muscle pain
Hepatitis B	Hepatitis virus B (Dane particle)	liver	same as above plus polyarthritis, skin rashes
Herpesvirus types 1 and 2	Herpes simplex virus types 1 and 2	mouth, lips, anus, penis	recurring lip and genital sores
Condylomata Acuminata	(virus)	anus	painful warty growth
Candidiasis	*Candida albicans* (yeast)	genital tract, alimentary canal	skin eruptions on buttocks, pneumonia
Acquired immuno-deficiency disease (A.I.D.)	unknown	B and T lympho-cytes	breakdown of immune system
Kaposi's sarcoma	unknown	skin and lymph glands	fever, cancerous tumors on body, swollen lymph glands
Pneumocystis carinii pneumonia	*Pneumoncystis carinii* (protozoan)	lungs	high fever, water-filled lungs
Toxoplasmosis	*Toxoplasma gondii*	central nervous system, spleen, liver	ulcerated sores of infected organs
Cryptococcosis	*Cryptococcus neoformans* (fungus)	meninges, lungs, joints, skin	nodular lesions or abscesses, meningitis

Glossary

acquired immune deficiency syndrome (AIDS): a disease characterized by the collapse of the immune system.

alopecia: loss of hair due to infection or a nervous condition.

aneurysm: bubbling out of an arterial wall.

antibiotic: a chemical extracted from fungus plants that destroys other microorganisms.

antibody: a protein molecule formed in the blood that reacts against a specific organism or protein.

ARC: AIDS-related complex.

arthritis: inflammation of muscle tissue or of a joint.

B cells: white blood cells that produce antibodies that fight off foreign viruses and bacteria.

bacillus (pl. bacilli): rod-shaped bacteria.

bacterium (pl. bacteria): single-celled microscopic plant; some species infectious to man and other organisms.

birth-control pills: sex-hormone preparations that prevent ovulation.

carrier: a person who transmits disease without having the symptoms of the disease.

capillary: the smallest of the blood vessels that connect arteries to veins.

causative agent: any organism that causes a disease.

cervix: the lower end of the uterus; passageway for sperm.

chancre: the primary lesion (ulcer) of syphilis.

chancroid: a venereal disease caused by Ducrey's bacillus.

Chlamydia trachomatis: the rickettsia that causes lympho-granuloma venereum.

communicable: capable of being spread from one person to another.

congenital: existing at birth.

contagious: capable of being spread from person to person.

crabs: lice that infest pubic hair and skin.

cytomegalovirus: a type of herpesvirus that destroys tissues in infants.

diagnosis: determination of the nature of disease.

DNA (deoxyribonucleic acid): a nucleic acid that carries hereditary information.

Donovan body: causative organism of granuloma inguinale.

Ducrey bacillus: popular term for causative organism of chancroid; also known as *Hemophilus ducreyi.*

elephantiasis: a disease in which body parts become grotesquely enlarged because of blockage of the lymphatic system.

epidemic: a particular disease that affects a large number of people in a given area.

epidemiologist: a scientist who specializes in the study of epidemics.

Frei test: the laboratory procedure for diagnosing lymphogranuloma venereum.

genitals: external sex organs.

germ: any organism or particle that enters the body and causes disease.

gonorrhea: most common venereal disease in the United States, characterized by pus formation and inflammation of the urethra or vagina. Street terms: clap, morning drop, the drip, a dose, strain, gleet, morning dew.

gonococcus: *Neisseria gonorrhoeae,* causative organism of gonorrhea.

granuloma inguinale: a venereal disease characterized by ulcerated lesions of the groin area.

gumma: an abscess caused by syphilitic infection.

Hemophilus decreyi: the causative organism of chancroid.

herpes simplex virus: the causative organism of fever blisters and gemota; herpes.

herpes genitalis: a virus disease of the genitals.

heterosexual: exhibiting sexual attraction for the opposite sex.

HIV: human immunodeficiency virus.

homosexual: exhibiting sexual attraction for one of the same sex.

host: the organism in which a parasite lives.

immune system: lymphocytes produced by lymph glands and bone marrow, which produce protective proteins that prevent disease.

infectious: referring to a disease caused by an invading organism.

intercourse: coitus, placement of the hardened penis into the vagina.

latent: hidden; present, but not visible.

lesion: a sore, may be ulcerated.

lymph: a clear watery fluid that bathes the body tissue.

lymph nodes: small, oval-shaped glands through which lymph filters.

lymphocyte: a special type of white blood cell that produces antibodies.

lymphogranuloma venereum: a venereal disease caused by a virus; results in ulceration of the genitals.

marker: a disease that signals the collapse of the immune system.

microorganism: any organism too small to be seen by the naked eye.

monilia: *(Candida albicans)* a yeast infection causing itching and inflammation of the genitals.

mucous membrane: thin, delicate tissue that forms the lining of the body cavities including the mouth, rectum, vagina, and urethra.

Neisseria gonorrhoeae: the causative organism of gonorrhea; known also as gonococcus.

nonspecific urethritis: unclassified group of infections of uncertain cause affecting the genital organs of both sexes.

opportunistic organism: a germ that infects the human body only when the immune system does not function.

paresis: paralysis resulting from untreated syphilis.

pathogenic: capable of causing disease.

penicillin: antibacterial drug used in the treatment of many infectious diseases.

penicillin-resistant gonorrhea: a type of gonorrhea produced by a bacterial strain that is able to destroy penicillin.

penicillinase: a penicillin-destroying enzyme.

penis: external sex organ of the male.

perinatal: occurring at the time of birth.

peritonitis: infection or inflammation of the abdominal cavity.

physiology: the study of the function of a living organism or its organs.

Pneumocystis carinii: an infectious protozoan causing pneumonia.

postnatal: occurring after birth.

promiscuous: engaging in frequent, indiscriminate sexual intercourse.

protist: a one-celled organism.

reproduction: process of conception, pregnancy, and birth.

retrovirus: an RNA virus.

sarcoma: a slow-growing cancerous tumor.

scabies: disease caused by infestation with a mite *(Sarcoptes scabiei).*

serum: the liquid part of the blood minus blood cells and clotting elements.

spirochete: the causative organism of syphilis; also known as *Treponema pallidum.*

syphilis: a venereal disease caused by the spirochete *T. pallidum,* transmitted through sexual intercourse. Street names: the lues, pox, old Joe, siff, haircut, bad blood.

T-helper cells: white blood cells that help the B cells to direct the body's immune activities.

testicles: the sperm-producing organs of the male, carried in the scrotum outside the body.

tetracycline: antibiotic used in the treatment of diseases that are resistant to penicillin.

Treponema pallidum: the spirochete that causes syphilis.

trichomoniasis: vaginal infection caused by a protozoan, *Trichomonas vaginalis,* producing an irritating discharge; carried by a male partner who has no symptoms.

ulceration: a running, open sore.

urethra: passageway through which urine passes from the bladder to the outside of the body.

vagina: passageway in the female from the outside of the body to the uterus; serves as the birth canal.

vaginitis: inflammation of vaginal tissues caused by a venereal yeast infection.

venereal diseases: numerous diseases spread through sexual intercourse or other sexual contact.

virion: a single virus.

Wassermann test: blood test to determine the presence of syphilis.

Bibliography

American Council on Science and Health. *11 Answers About AIDS*. Summit, N.J., 1987.

Cahill, Kevin M. (ed). *The AIDS Epidemic*. New York: St. Martin's Press, 1983.

Fromer, Margot J. *AIDS*. New York: Pinnacle Books, Inc., 1983.

Hamilton, Richard. *The Herpes Book*. Los Angeles: J. P. Tarcher, Inc. (distributed by Houghton Mifflin, Boston), 1981.

Ma, Pearl, and Armstrong, Donald. *The Acquired Immune Deficiency Syndrome and Infections of Homosexual Men*. New York: Yorke Medical Books, 1984.

Ulene, Art. *Safe Sex in a Dangerous World*. New York: Vintage Books, 1987

Sexually Transmitted Disease News Letters. City of New York, Bureau of Venereal Disease Control, 1981-82.

U.S. Department of Health, Education, and Welfare. *The Eradication of Syphilis*. Washington, D.C.: Public Health Service Publ. 918.

Articles

Altman, Lawrence K. "New Homosexual Disorder Worries Health Officials." *New York Times*, May 11, 1982.

———. "Federal Official Says He Believes Cause of AIDS Has Been Found." *New York Times*, April 22, 1984.

———. "New U.S. Report Names Virus That May Cause AIDS." *New York Times*, April 24, 1984.

Boffey, Philip M. "A Likely AIDS Cause, But Still No Cure." *New York Times*, April 29, 1984.

Brody, Jane. "Herpes Now Blamed for More Illness Than Any Other Human Viruses." *New York Times*, May 4, 1982.

———. "Infection Linked to Sex Surpasses Gonorrhea." *New York Times*, June 5, 1984.

Clark, Matt, and Gosnell, Mariana. "Diseases That Plague Gays." *Newsweek*, December 21, 1981.

Edelson, Edward. "See Hope in Herpes Drug Test." *Daily News*, July 24, 1982.

Edelson, Edward. "Researchers Pin Hopes on 2 New Herpes Drugs." *Daily News*, March 24, 1983.

———. "Eye Blood Marker as Help in AIDS Fight." *Daily News*, June 8, 1984.

Feldman, Yehudi M., M.D. "Kaposi's Sarcome." *Medical Society of Kings County Bulletin*, March, 1982.

Giordano, Mary Ann. "AIDS Cases Zoom in U.S." *Daily News*, September, 1983.

Laskin, Daniel. "The Herpes Syndrome." *New York Times Magazine*, February 21, 1982.

Lynch, Eileen. "The Herpes Threat: Why Casual Sex Isn't Casual Anymore." *McCalls*, September, 1982.

McClarrin, Otto. "Herpes: New Virus of Love." *New York Recorder*, July 17, 1982.

Randal, Judith. "Doc Cites Virus in AIDS." *Daily News*, April 23, 1984.

———. "Dual AIDS Discoveries Answer Some Questions." *Daily News*, April 29, 1984.

VerMeulen, Michael. "The Gay Plague." *New York*, May 31, 1982.

"U.S. Medical Study Singles Out a Man Who Carried AIDS." *New York Times*, March 27, 1984.

Index

A
acquired immune deficiency syndrome (AIDS), 59-70, 71, 94, 104
acyclovir, 50-52
alopecia, 18
amebiasis, 85, 86-87, 88
amebic dysentery, 87
antibody, 17-18, 62, 64, 66
antigen, 83, 84
anus, 47, 61
azidothymidine (AZT), 71

B
bacteria, 13, 33, 38, 41-42, 64, 77, 78, 85
B cells, 62, 66
birth control, 91
    pill, 4, 103
bisexual, 61, 66
blindness, 23, 26, 35, 57, 94, 104
blood, 16, 17, 33, 61, 62, 66, 104
    donation, 70, 104
    transfusion, 61, 67, 70

C
cancer, 48, 65, 74, 103
Candida albicans, 64, 76
carrier, disease, 50, 83, 103
cervix, 11, 34, 35, 37-38, 48, 78
chancre, 16, 97, 99
chancroid, 3, 77-78
Chlamydia trachomatis, 78, 104
condom, 12, 71, 99, 102, 104
condylomata acuminatum, 73-74
congenital syphilis, 24, 25-28
cryptosporidiasis, 64
cytomegalovirus (CMV), 43, 46, 53-58

D
dementia, 69
deoxyribonucleic acid (DNA), 41, 43, 44, 45, 48, 51, 54, 68
disease
    contagious, 4, 15
    infectious, 4, 18, 31, 41, 81, 88, 92
    intestinal, 85-89
    opportunistic, 63-64, 66
drug abuse, intravenous, 61, 67, 71, 81

E
Epstein-Barr virus (EBV), 46, 55
erythromycin, 28, 29

F
fallopian tubes, 10, 34, 37, 38, 73, 78, 101
fertilization, 10, 11
Frei test, 79

G
genital herpes, 3, 47-50, 54, 71, 103-104
    See also venereal herpes.
genitals, 7, 16, 41, 46, 51, 78, 79, 99
giardiasis, 85, 88
gonorrhea, 3, 4, 31-37, 49, 55, 71, 77, 84, 94, 100-103
granuloma inguinale, 3, 79

H
herpes simplex (HSV), 46-47, 51
herpesvirus, 45-47, 50, 54, 56, 64
herpes-zoster, 46
hepatitis, 64, 79-84
homosexual, 61, 63, 65, 66, 78, 82, 84, 86, 88, 95-96, 103, 104
human immunodeficiency virus (HIV), 61, 66-68

I
immune system, 44, 61, 62-65, 66, 67, 69, 78
infectious mononucleosis, 46, 55
intrauterine device (IUD), 37

K
Kaposi's sarcoma (KS), 65-66

L
latent syphilis, 21, 24
late syphilis, 21-23, 24
lymphogranuloma venereum, 3, 78

M
marker disease, 65-66
meningitis, 64
metronidazole, 73

117